# It's Our Own Knowledge

370
.19
09713
O59
Cop.1

# It's Our Own Knowledge
## Labour, Public Education & Skills Training

Julie Davis ◆ John Huot ◆ Nancy Jackson
Richard Johnston ◆ Doug Little ◆ George Martell
Penny Moss ◆ Doug Noble ◆ Jim Turk ◆ Gord Wilson

Papers presented at the
Ontario Federation of Labour
Conference on Education and Training:
Labour Issues for the 1990s,
Toronto, May, 1989.

Ontario Federation of Labour Conference on Education and Training: Labour Issues for the 1990s (1989: Toronto, Ont.)

It's our own knowledge

Papers presented at the Ontario Federation of Labour Conference on Education and Training: Labour Issues for the 1990s, Toronto, May, 1989.

ISBN 0-921908-03-2

1. Working class – Education – Ontario – Congresses.
2. Educational equalization – Ontario – Congresses.
3. Education – Ontario – Aims and objectives – Congresses.
I. Davis, Julie, 1947- . II. Our Schools/Our Selves Education Foundation. III. Title.

LC5054.2.0505 1989    370.19'09713    C90-093133-7

This book is published jointly by Our Schools/Our Selves Education Foundation, 1698 Gerrard Street East, Toronto, Ontario, M4L 2B2 and Garamond Press, 67A Portland Street, Toronto, Ontario, M5V 2M9.

For subscribers to **Our Schools/Our Selves: a magazine for Canadian education activists,** this is issue #8, the last issue of volume 1.

The subscription series **Our Schools/Our Selves** (ISSN 0840-7339) is published 8 times a year. Second class mail registration number 8010.

Design and art work by **Goodness Graphics**.
Managing editor: Deborah Wise Harris

Printed in Canada by Del Charters Litho, Brampton, Ontario.
Copyright © Our Schools/Our Selves Education Foundation
November 1989

# Table of Contents

**Preface** *i*
Gord Wilson

**Introduction** *1*
Jim Turk

1. **Getting An Education The Hard Way** *9*
Gord Wilson

2. **Labelling, Streaming, & Programming of Working Class Kids In School** *19*
George Martell

3. **Keeping Workers In Their Place: The Role Of The Community College** *31*
John Huot

4. **Equal Outcomes** *39*
Penny Moss

5. **Priorities For De-Streaming And Improving Working Class Success** *43*
Doug Little

6. **Changing Education Through Politics** *51*
Richard Johnston

7. **High Tech Skills: The Corporate Assault On The Hearts And Minds of Union Workers** *59*
Doug Noble

8. **Training For Workers, Not For Bosses** *81*
Nancy Jackson

9. **Taking Charge Of Our Future** *99*
Julie Davis

**Appendices** *107*

**Where We Stand:**
*Submissions To The Ontario Select Committee On Education From The Ontario Federation of Labour*

# *Preface*

This book reflects the Ontario Federation of Labour's growing commitment to improving the education and training available to working people in Ontario.

We are concerned about what happens to our children in school and to our co-workers in the workplace.

We want education and training that encourages critical thinking, not uncritical compliance with authority. We want education that is oriented to the life-long needs of people, not to the immediate economic desires of employers. Our educational system's goal must not be the mirage of equality of opportunity. We want equality of results in which all people will be better able to live fulfilling and meaningful lives at home, in the community and at work.

We are committed to working with teachers, community groups and others to make this kind of educational system a reality.

The articles in this book offer a challenge. They reflect our experience of the problems in education and training, and they present our thoughts about the kinds of solutions we want.

We hope this book will spark discussions about education and training in homes and workplaces across the country. We also hope it makes clear that the labour movement views education and training as principal issues for us now and in the future.

*Gord Wilson*
*President*
*Ontario Federation of Labour*

# Introduction

*Jim Turk*

## Good Public Education: A Key Issue For Labour

In the mid-1880's, the Toronto Trades Assembly, like other labour organizations in Canada, made public education a key issue.

Labour wanted good, accessible education for everybody. It called for free school books, school scholarships, preservation of kindergarten.

It attacked Upper Canada College as a class institution.

It demanded a levelling up of women teachers' salaries, urged teachers to form a union and strongly supported the Women Teachers' Association.

It refused to endorse the call for one national non-sectarian school system, but it objected to the use of the Bible as a textbook and argued against dogmatic and sectarian religious teaching.

It condemned the expulsion of a student because "of his fondness for dime novels".

It opposed manual training in schools, but favoured technical schools. Manual training was seen as giving employers a pool of semi-skilled strikebreakers, but technical education would allow workers to become skilled tradespeople.

It called for a better class of teachers in night school and attacked reductions in funding for libraries.

Access; opposition to private schools; good pay and working conditions for teachers; recognition of historical commitments to separate schools but opposition to religious dogma; respect for popular culture as well as classical; emphasis on practical education but not narrow vocational training; good instructors and materials for life-long learning – these were the issues addressed by labour in the 1880's, and they have continued to be central to trade unions' concerns about education over the intervening 100 years.

Education is a fundamental issue for trade unions; as it is for the whole of the working class. Education is supposed to be a vehicle by which equality is available in our society. From the outset, workers saw that the educational system also could be the vehicle by which they were kept in their place.

This contradiction between the goals and the reality of the educational system has been a constant theme in labour's discussion of education.

Almost exactly 100 years after the Toronto Trades Assembly developed most of its policy on public education, the Ontario Federation of Labour held a convention at which education policy was a central issue.

## *A Renewed Commitment*

The Convention debated and passed a policy paper entitled *Life-Long Learning* and charted a course of action for the rest of the 1980's. A central concern was bluntly stated: "Our school system operates against the interests of the children of working people."

A number of necessary changes were identified: affordable, high-quality child care for low and middle income families; elimination of streaming in elementary and secondary school; broad-based, learner-centred adult education; greater worker and community involvement in the operation and policy-making of educational system; opposition to funding for private schools; vocational education that is worker-centred; paid educational leave as a right; enhanced literacy and second-language opportunities; and a more activist role for labour in public educational matters.

One consequence of that review was a renewed commitment by the Ontario Federation of Labour to act as an advocate for the interests of workers and their children in the publicly-funded educational system. A second was to initiate labour's own adult basic education program.

## *The Issue Of Streaming*

As the trade union movement identified its current concerns with regard to schooling, none was seen to be more important than streaming. This is the practice by which students are divided into informal or formal groups based on someone's judgment of their abilities.

It begins in Ontario (as elsewhere) almost as soon as the child enters school. The groupings tend to be more informal in the early years. Reading groups given innocent names like "wrens", "robins" and "bluebirds" mark the beginning of the labelling and sorting of children from which few will ever escape.

This is allegedly done to help every child reach his or her "full potential". But the results are quite different. In study after study, a common fact is found: grouping reflects social standing more than any measure of achievement or ability. The bottom-stream programs in any school board are almost entirely populated by working class children.

The same holds true in "learning disability" classes and other "special education" programs except those for the physiologically disabled. It is the children of workers who are stuck here "for their own good", and usually, for their lifetime.

This is not a simple matter. Many working class children do well in school, and many are in advanced streams. But why are only workers' children in the bottom streams?

Are working class children less able, or is Ontario's educational system geared to maintain the advantages of the advantaged? We have no doubt about the answer.

Schooling has helped enough working class children to get ahead that most workers see it as their best chance to provide a better life for their children. The "success" of the few obscures the reality that most come out of school at roughly the same social level as they entered.

Not only is the reality obscured, but it is used to blame the victims. It is individual failing, disability, lack of attention or bad attitude that are used to account for who does well in school. Most educational authorities would have us ignore the fact that, overall, social status is the best predictor of who does "well" in school, who is put in an academic stream, who goes to university and who gets the best jobs.

For the trade union movement, equality does not refer to the elusive "equality of opportunity." It refers to the much more tangible "equality of outcome." As long as social status is a good predictor of who does well in school, we know the school system is failing. As long as it is almost entirely working class kids who are in the bottom streams, we know there is a need for fundamental change.

## *Where Labour Stands*

In wrestling with streaming and related issues, the Ontario Federation of Labour has articulated its position in a series of presentations to the Ontario Legislature's Select Committee on Education.

The three submissions are attached as appendices. The first (Appendix 1) addresses what we see to be the goals of education. Broadly stated, these are "to equip everyone with the basic ability to acquire information, to reason clearly, to think critically, to communicate one's ideas effectively and to try to put one's ideas and knowledge into practice."

In the second submission (Appendix 2), we propose solutions to the problems of public schools – abolition of streaming; introduction of a core curriculum; new approaches to pedagogy and teacher training; better teaching conditions and materials; greater concern for real accountability and an increased role for the community.

In the third submission (Appendix 3), we discuss school funding and distinguish labour's criticism of public education from the increasingly fashionable criticism by business and government.

Unlike these organizations, our commitment to public education is deepened by our criticism. We feel that more resources must be put into education to allow it to grow stronger and to better meet the needs we have identified. But funding should be removed from the backs of property taxpayers and be raised through a more progressive provincial income tax.

## Putting Philosophy Into Practice

At the same time as discussing educational policy with the Ontario government, the OFL has been attempting to put its educational philosophy into practice.

Starting last September, the OFL and its member unions set up their Basic Education for Skills Training (BEST) project. BEST offers French and English literacy and second language programs in more than 100 workplaces across the province. All programs are delivered by specially trained rank-and-file workers in their own workplaces.

It is the Federation's intention to make this a model of our conception of adult education. The approach is genuinely learner-centred – one in which the participants help set the objectives, participate in the development of the learning materials, and help evaluate the success of the program both individually and collectively.

We want our own educational practice to help guide the policy and practical advice we give others.

## Reaching Out To The Community

In addition to advocacy and offering our own programs, we want to reach out to others in the community who share our concerns about education. To start that process, the OFL hosted a conference on educational issues in May, 1989. The conference was attended by 200 trade unionists from across the province along with teachers, and other community activists.

This book contains the papers presented at the conference. They reflect a diversity of viewpoints, but share a common objective of promoting a strong, more accessible and more egalitarian educational system.

OFL President Gordon Wilson opened the conference by relating his own experiences of school as a working class boy in a relatively affluent school in London, Ontario. Gord's story proved remarkably similar to that of others at the conference who had had a working class background. His frankness set a tone for honest appraisal of educational issues.

George Martell and John Huot followed with a discussion of how working class students are streamed in elementary and secondary school and in college. Their clear identification of the problems set the stage for the subsequent presentations about solutions.

Penny Moss reminded us that almost all children prove to be excellent learners before ever entering school, and come out of school much more unequal than when they entered. Doug Little drew from his experience as a teacher to identify what can be done in the classroom. Richard Johnson, the NDP's education critic, related his own school experiences and reflected on what is necessary politically to bring change.

After leaving school, most people must undertake significant learning tasks as part of their jobs. Few receive any formal training at work. In recent years, it has become fashionable to stress the importance of skills training for Canada's future.

American writer and educator, Doug Noble, asked

...why, in an increasingly high-tech work world that displaces or de-skills more and more workers every week, do corporate pronouncements endlessly promote sophisticated education and training as the key to competitiveness and worker survival? What do they really want? What is their agenda?

His chilling answer should be carefully considered by every worker in this country.

Nancy Jackson explored what can be done to make training benefit workers. Her proposals offer a challenge for the future.

OFL Secretary-Treasurer Julie Davis summarized the conference. She drew together the presentations and renewed labour's commitment to work aggressively for educational reform.

These papers, and the response in the workshops that followed them, made clear that the labour movement has not become cynical about public education. We continue to feel that the public educational system can be different. It can be a vehicle for equality. It can promote progressive change. It can allow people to learn throughout their lives. It can help empower people instead of disabling them.

## INTRODUCTION

Our brothers and sisters in the 1880's were trying to bring reality closer to their vision. We continue that mission today. We firmly believe that the problems of the educational system will not change without unions – the principal organizations of the working class – playing a leading role. That role is not just to identify the problems, but also to help identify the solutions and to struggle to bring them into being.

*Jim Turk was Research Director for the United Electrical Workers and is currently Education Director for the Ontario Federation of Labour.*

# Chapter 1
## Getting An Education The Hard Way

*Gord Wilson*

On reflection, looking back upon my educational experiences, I was far more compromised in school than I ever have been by any manager or government official.

My formal education experience was not very pleasant, and I think my experience has been shared by many others. When I left school at a very young age – I was a few weeks short of my sixteenth birthday – I had a feeling that I had somehow failed: that I failed myself by not making it to the end, and that I had not lived up to my family's expectations of what I would achieve in the education system.

I think I now understand what really did happen to me, and I suspect, like all of us, that I was partly culpable. But it was the manner in which the system was designed that really created the problem or, at least, the environment which had an impact on me. Quite frankly, I don't think I am any different than most trade union activists.

I can recall a few years ago on the then UAW staff, I conducted a poll among the staff members and discovered that slightly more than half of them had been thrown out of school. There was a consistency to why they left. For most of them, it was not so much economic reasons – that's a part of it – but the reality was most of them were thrown out because school authorities said they were uncooperative, they were incorrigible. I suspect that a lot of people in this room had similar experiences.

## *Class Realities*

I want to tell you a little a bit about my background. I was born in Belleville in June, 1939. My father came home in September and announced to my mother that he had sold the car and joined the Navy. She almost killed him. At the age of two, I moved from Belleville – that hot-bed of social democracy – to London, Ontario. When we arrived we all moved in with my mother's sister, and we stayed there until my father came back from overseas in 1946.

With dad at home, we packed off to the north end of London, in the Huron-Adelaide area. This part of the world was mostly pasture with a few veteran-land-act homes scattered about. These homes were quickies they put together cheaply but sold for about $8000 – which was a fortune in those days. Rents, though, were often exorbitant and it made sense for my parents to buy a house. I remember their mortgage payment was $29.30 a month. Most of you will spend that in the bar tonight.

Still, my parents and others like them often had difficulty trying to get that amount together. I'm not pleading poverty, but I don't want to neglect it either. I can recall my father worked in a job as a "stationary engineer" which was then a nice way of saying he took care of the boilers. I could always tell when payday was. (Dad was paid once a month.) I could read the calendar, which helped, but the real sign was that the last couple of days before payday the sandwiches I took to school were white sugar or brown sugar. That may explain why some of us look the way we do today. You could always tell the day after payday because you got a bacon sandwich or something like that. That was really the big thing of the month. I don't want to dwell on our poverty, but in terms of where kid's minds are, these were important things.

I wasn't alone in this either. Our veterans-land-act subdivision was working class and poor. Most of the vets didn't have much to call their own. There weren't too many rich kids' families where the fathers went off and really took a gun out. These guys rarely went to where the real war was.

I was also raised a Roman Catholic and went to a Roman Catholic school – I actually did have scruples at one point in my life – and this was important in making me a lot clearer about the class I was raised in. Our area was included in St. Michael's Parish in the north end of London. This parish was the only Catholic parish in the north end, and mostly it was filled with fairly wealthy families. There were a few exceptions who broke through the social barrier by having the distinction of living in the VLA area or down lower in the Oxford-Piccadilly-Adelaide area, which is another working class area. As a result, in our Catholic school, there were a lot of rich kids, whose dads had often made their money not long ago, and there were five or six of us working class kids.

## *Looking Through Us*

When I think back – I didn't know it then, but I know now – there were a lot of unpleasant subtleties in the way I was dealt with in school. I'm not whining about this, but I think it is important to realize.

We were different, very different from the comfortable majority, which surrounded us. We were an economic minority, and didn't receive much encouragement to pursue academic endeavours in the school. In fact, they hardly recognized we were there. They had to deal with us, of course, but nobody got very excited about our presence. Mostly, it seems to me, they looked through us.

There was a sense that we somehow would be in school for a period of time – floating unattached – and then pass on to somewhere unknown at the end of Grade 8.

I think it's fair to say that my friends and I were not any more mischievous than most kids are in grade school. Okay, maybe a bit more. Sometimes we got into trouble. When someone went after us, we dug in a little bit, and got ourselves into more trouble.

None of it seemed very serious at this time. It still doesn't today. But it caused my family a considerable amount of anguish. My father was stretched trying to make a living. My mother took care of the home and was held responsible for my school success. She did not work at a paying job. Those were in the days when working class families actually could survive on one salary. It's different from today when you have to have two salaries to exist.

The anguish for my mother was real. She wasn't prepared for my disinterest and hostility of the school. She was a woman born in the 1920's into a very traditional working class society where class distinctions were deeply felt. She was raised in a place called Dunbarton which is just outside of Glasgow in Scotland. In this working class area each new child might automatically be stamped "Labour Party" on their ass – you never forgot who you voted for – but children like my mum also learned to respect their "betters", especially in places like school. My mum learned there were strict rules you observed: what the church said you observed, what the establishment said you went along with. On the other side of the fence, once you were in a strike situation, you also didn't go out and rock the boat. For my mum, the union, and the community that supported it, was another establishment to be obeyed.

So, the troubles at school caused my mother all kinds of anguish. My reports would come in, and I would get detentions and extra homework. My objective was to have no homework. I was fairly successful at it most of the time.

The highlight of my school year was summer vacation.

## *Money Talking*

A lot of the activities around the school had a cost factor attached to them. These costs often excluded us from participation. A really big weekend for me was when I got an allowance of 25 cents on Friday night and came home with that same allowance in my pocket on Sunday night because the cops missed us going over the fence at the dance park. They did not catch me at the school dance either. We had two guys sucker the two guards at the door so we could slip by them and get in for free. We needed to hold on to our 25 cents; there were other things we wanted to spend it on in the next week, like cigarettes.

In the school yard there was a kind of solidarity among the kids who came from the excluded working class families. And our friendships spilled over into the classroom. We hung together, mostly in silence and sometimes in horseplay, when the class talked about things like current events. It was different for us. While others mentioned how they "went here ... went there," we all knew we had never been anywhere. It was a big deal for us if we went to the swimming pool at the nearby park. We didn't want to talk about that, so we didn't talk at all.

There were also some attitude problems on the part of some teachers. I don't want to make too much of it, but there were several teachers who were always trying to make it up the social ladder, to gain acceptance within the largely well-to-do community of our school's parents. These teachers were much more attentive to some of the kids who came from the higher level of the society than to us working class kids. Of course, this approach was not true of all teachers, but it wasn't an uncommon experience.

## *Dennis McDermott: Choirs and Leftovers*

My experience is not a lot different from that of many people, and for most of us it leaves a bitter taste.

Let me give another example. Dennis McDermott, the former head of the CLC and before that the Autoworkers, has an extroverted personality. I do not want to disparage the man because he is an ambassador to Ireland, and, who knows, I might get an invitation to visit him one day, and I would not want to do anything to ruin that.

But in fairness to Dennis, I had many years with him when he was a director of the Autoworkers, where he encouraged us all in creative and militant unionism.

Dennis told me a story one night at Port Elgin about being a schoolboy in Liverpool. (He was born in Ireland but he was raised in Liverpool.)

One of the big events in the Liverpool school system at that time was for kids involved in school choirs to win an invitation to sing in Westminster Abbey. If your school got picked to do that it was quite an honour.

Dennis was in a choir at his school, and it was picked to sing in Westminster Abbey. Of course, everyone associated with the choir was extremely proud of the honour.

In order to appropriately present themselves at Westminster Abbey, Dennis and his choirmates were each told that they had to have grey slacks and blue blazers. (I assume there were no young women involved. As Dennis tells the story, I do not think there were.)

Dennis came from a very poor economic beginning, and his family did not have the money to buy him a jacket. Nor was one to be found through the usual system of relatives, neighbours and friends. The result was that some other substitute was found, and he piled onto this bus as did all of the other kids. They went trumbling off to Westminster Abbey.

Imagine, now, all these kids – thirteen, fourteen years of age – and how excited they would all be. When they arrived at Westminster Abbey and began to disembark from the bus, the choirmaster stopped Dennis and said, "McDermott stand aside." Poor Dennis said his reaction was "I don't remember doing anything this week, I'm not sure what this one's about. Maybe I'm going to win something this time."

When all of the kids had departed from the bus and headed into the Abbey, the choirmaster said to McDermott, "You are inappropriately dressed. You do not meet the standards. You cannot participate. Get back on the bus."

Well, I can tell you I think that experience – whether Dennis is prepared to admit it or not – is probably why Dennis McDermott now spends a considerable amount of his income on clothes. I remember being in an airport with Dennis years ago when he spent more on tie than I spent on a suit.

I will tell you another thing, because psychologically it fits into all of this: Dennis never eats leftovers. I do not know whether some of you in the Autoworkers are aware of that or not. Again, I think it comes from his beginnings.

I had a dog called "Scampy", and Dennis used to like barbecued steaks. I use the word "steaks" ill-advisedly; they were closer to roasts. He would buy these steaks, and he would always eat the eye out of them. He would never eat the outside of it. When we used to have dinner at Port Elgin, he would come over with these pieces of meat because he liked dogs, and he would say "this is for Scampy." After this happened a couple of times, I said to my wife Bonnie, "To hell with Scampy, we'll take them ourselves!"

McDermott might have paid a lot of attention to his dress code and spent a lot of effort getting to his prime cuts, but I want to tell you, all you had to do was be snotty or arrogant around McDermott or put your nose up in front of him, and war was on. I really do believe that it is experiences of humiliation like this, which so many of us have had in school, which led Dennis into his values.

## *No Looking Back*

When I went to high school, I did not get along a lot better than in elementary school. The only good memory I can recall was being on the high school football team. When I think about why I felt good about football, the pleasure of the sport itself wasn't the only factor. The football team was probably the only place in the school in which I got treated equally to the rich kids.

When you think back about these things, you realize you didn't think too much about them at the time, but they do effect your attitudes in later life.

My last school experience (and I want to close on this one) really turned my head to understanding the social class I come from.

We had a kid in the school who came from a very well-to-do family. I was about 15 years of age at the time and so was this kid. He was the kind of kid who always tried to blame someone else whenever he got into trouble – whether he was at home, in the neighbourhood or at school. He whined a lot. And the whining seemed to work for him.

One day, during the winter, we were fooling around with a bunch of sleds and toboggans by St. Joseph's Hospital, which used to be a big building beside a big ditch. The ditch was a great place to horse around in. This kid came racing down the hill in his new sled, and he lost control of it, whacked it into a tree and just shattered it.

Well, I want to tell you, it was a great day for us, we just sat there and cheered and thought it could not happen to a better fellow. Then we went on about our business.

When I went to school the following week, however, I discovered that that was not the end of the incident. The principal of the high school – it was Catholic Central High School in London – called three of us into the office and asked us why we had beaten this kid up and broken his toboggan. We said we did not do it. He said the boy and his parents had been in to see him and he told us: "They made the accusation, which I believe, that you kids did beat him up and broke up his toboggan." We said, "No, we did not."

For a number of days – for at least a week, it seems to me, or a week and a half – there was a fairly constant interrogation in the principal's office. We were called in separately, and we were called back in together. They kept on grinding, grinding, grinding. We kept on saying we did not do it, the little bugger did it himself. But the grinding finally got to the other two guys, who were intellectually brighter than I was. They decided they had to get this thing off our backs – so they said, "Yup, we did it."

The principal's reaction apparently was that's good, you're reprimanded, you'll serve these detentions, and that's the end of it.

When I came in, he said, "You did it." I said, "No I didn't." He said, "Your two friends said you did it." I said, "Well, they may have, but I didn't." He said, "They said they did it." I said, "Well, I was there, and they didn't do it."

He said, "If you continue to lie, it shows a failing in character, and if you continue on this course then ultimately you are going to be expelled from this school." With that I said, "Thank you very much, I quit." I was about three months short of my 16th birthday. As I walked out, I'll never forget, there was a glass panel in the centre of the principal's door, and I winged that sucker as hard as I could behind me coming out. I remember the glass flying all over the place, and I said to myself, "Wilson, keep going, it's all over." I walked out the door, and it was the last time I was ever in the place. There was no looking back.

## *Working Class Kids And The System*

On reflection, what seems important for many of us who are in this room today is that we went through an application of class distinction in our education. We experienced a system that was designed to maintain, promote and advance those who begin from a position of privilege.

For most of us, there was, I think, a question of family economic situation. Like many of you, as a working kid, from a working family, I had to have a part-time job if I wanted pocket money. So I went out and found one. Many of you, I'm sure, did that as well – whether it was delivering papers before the sun came up or doing something in the corner store or delivering for drugstores riding your bicycle in snowstorms. We all did it. We also knew we had to find a summer job if we wanted to have money to play around with when we went back to school.

On top of that, we all had chores that had to be done around the house. I did not get out of the house until I did my chores. I had to wash, wax and polish the bathroom and kitchen floors. (We did not have the high-tech stuff you have today where you just wash. In those days, after washing, you had to wax with an old nylon and then polish.) I also had to do the gardening. Only after that could I get the hell out of the place.

We did not have any vacations to go to. On the other hand, when I think back to those kids, who came from reasonably well-off families, they often took jobs on a part-time basis during the summer. But for them it was not an economic decision they were making. They had a choice. They felt like doing it. If they didn't feel like doing it who gets excited? They didn't have to worry about it. It was not a necessity. Not too many of them had chores to do around the house, especially when there was hired help available. And they went on a lot of vacations.

They were also expected to do well at school. And they

expected it themselves. It was in the air they breathed at home and in school. It was their system. Whereas, with most of us, our parents simply had a great deal of hope that we were going to be higher in life than they had been able to be. But they didn't really expect it. Why should the system be different for their kids than it had been for themselves? And, as it turned out, it wasn't.

I think all of us in this room have shared, in one sense or another, some of the things I have talked to you about. That's the objective of the planners of this conference: that we should talk openly amongst each other about the kinds of experiences that we have had. I'll bet there are some incredible stories in this room of what people have done, and we need to share those with no embarrassment. We should have absolutely no shame attached to what happened to us at school, because I want to tell you, my friends, we did not fail the system, the system failed us.

*Gord Wilson, a former education director of the United Auto Workers, is now president of the Ontario Federation of Labour.*

# Chapter 2

# The Labelling, Streaming and Programming of Working Class Kids In School

### George Martell

How Gord Wilson approached his own experience of schooling, it seems to me, is how Labour generally ought to deal with the question of what happens to working class kids in school: an approach that is tough, unsentimental, and from the heart.

Looking out at the faces in this room it is clear that we all know that Gord got to the important truth about our schooling. It is a truth that has cut deeply into our lives, and we are very grateful to hear it spoken aloud, in public, for everyone to hear.

We also know, if Gord is right about what happened to most of us in school, much the same thing is going to happen or is already happening to our kids. The people who run our schools haven't stopped being hostile, not by any means, though their community P.R. may have become smoother over the years. We know now we can no longer hope, as we may have in the past, that our current school system will do well by our kids. Either we fight for a decent educational system, or they'll be hurt as much as we were. Maybe more.

My job this morning is to open up a broader discussion of this situation – the ways in which our elementary and secondary schools keep workers' kids in their place – and then consider what Labour's response ought to be.

## Keeping Workers' Kids At The Bottom

What are the means by which schools insure that our kids stay at the bottom of the educational system in preparation, it turns out, for their living and working at the bottom of the society when they leave school?

What we want to get at, in other words, is the institutional process Gord Wilson had to fight so hard against when he was a student some 30 years ago. And against which all of you have had to struggle.

Everyone here knows how hard it was to stand up for your dignity in school. You know especially how hard it was to keep faith with your intelligence, with your knowledge that you were as smart and as able as anyone else. This knowledge should be obvious when we look at this room full of union leaders who have proved their competence and their smarts in the real world. But to those who wield power in this society and who control its education and its media, working class intelligence is not one bit obvious – at least as it's portrayed to the public. The recognition of this intelligence is something you have had to fight for ever since you were kids.

For all of your lives you have had to go against the grain of what the society – and especially its school system – has told you about your capacity to understand and act upon the world. This judgement was not always on the surface, of course, but it was almost always there working against you as you grew up: "You don't have what it takes to make it in the world," it said, "you deserve to be in the bottom ranks of the society."

The basics of the process of keeping working class kids on the bottom, which Gord experienced, remain solidly entrenched in today's school. Only now the process is slipperier and sleazier. It's not so crude as it used to be. In some ways that makes it even harder for working people and their kids to get hold of and to fight. It is also a process that has become more all encompassing, filling up the nooks and crannies of the system, making it seem increasingly "natural".

Now, more than ever, what happens to working class kids in school is all being done "for their own good," as our educational administrators never cease pointing out to us. And in the last couple of decades the process is increasingly laid on by an army of test experts and psychometricians, social workers and psychologists, who come at workers and their kids with obscure scientific jargon about diagnosis and treatment and a lot of heavy rhetoric about a student's personal fulfillment in life. "We care about your kid", they say. "Don't you care?" they ask. "Don't you want what's best for your children, what will help them in the future?"

What do you say?

For a caring parent it is a bewildering situation. You want to do right by your kid, but every intuition you have tells you something is terribly wrong here.

What I want to say this morning, is that we have to trust our intuitions here. We have to start saying "NO" to this process and at the same time get down to the very difficult task of trying to figure out, much more precisely, what really is wrong here.

## *Labels, Streams, Programs*

There are, it seems to me, three main ways in which those who run our schools try to keep workers' kids at the bottom and which we, in turn, have to resist.

(These administrative and political initiatives are resisted, I want to add here, by lots of good teachers; the worst thing we can do is to scapegoat teachers for a system largely outside their control.)

The first thrust is the labelling – at different levels or degrees – of more and more working class kids as dumber and crazier than middle class and rich kids. "Dumb"/"smart", "crazy"/ "sane" are the two big category systems used to define kids, which are often linked together into one package when dealing with a kid. "Educationally retarded, with behavioural problems" to take a simple example. Usually there's a lot of fancy pseudo-scientific language in these definitions. Someone once figured out there were 52 euphemisms for "stupid".

Then there is the placement – or streaming – of these kids (defined as dumb and crazy in varying degrees) according to how dumb and crazy they are judged to be.

Finally, there is the programming that is laid on according to the labels.

These three system initiatives – labelling, streaming and programming – cover a lot of territory. I want to focus on two important elements within this territory, which connect directly with the issue of skills training, which you will be considering tomorrow and which are at core of the working class oppression in our schools.

(1) The process by which so many working class kids get to be labelled as not as smart as middle class and rich kids.

(2) The curriculum or program thrust that goes along with this understanding of who's intelligent and who's not.

## *Intelligence Labelling*

The intelligence label is the big label. It's the one that counts the most against our kids. The one that school officials tell us we can't do anything about. They shake their heads; they're sorry, of course. But "If your kid's stupid, he's stupid; if she's smart, she's smart. Nothing the school can do about that, is there? Don't blame us for poor marks."

So how do they decide if your kid's stupid or smart? There's an objective measure, you'll be pleased to know. It has to do with how well your kid does on certain tasks, like IQ tests, reading tests, and the repetition of various forms of mindless rote learning.

What these tasks are primarily about is your children's ability to hold unrelated facts or images in their heads and then carry out, as fast they can, a very shallow kind of formal logic. They can be asked to do this in a whole range of activities: putting shapes to shapes (as in the Raven IQ test), putting words to words (which I'll explain in a second), or completing fill-in-the-blanks/multiple-choice/true-and-false tests (like the tests in the Senior High School Chemistry and Physics Review that came down last week from the Ontario Ministry of Education, which are part of the big push for standardized tests we're seeing right across the country.)

Let me give you an example of putting words to words. It's in the form of a little kids' I.Q. test:

Imagine four boxed pictures: a butcher, a baker, a candlestick maker and a police officer. What, the kids are asked, do these figures have in common?

The right answer, for 2 points, is that they are all "men" or "people."

What the kids who got it right have done is to put words like butcher, baker, candlestick maker and police officer under the broader category of "men" or "people". They have, in this context, put words to a word. It is a narrow skill, learned quite explicitly in most middle class homes.

What many working class kids do in a test like this, unless they have been coached to do otherwise, is to express a social relationship between the people in the boxes. For example: "The policeman is chasing the other three men." or "The butcher got robbed, and the others are helping him." If you tip them off on the right answer, many will look at you as if you're crazy. "What kind of an answer is that?" you can hear them thinking. "We know they're men, or people. What's that got to do with anything?"

At the most fundamental level these kids are right. But they still get 0 out of 2.

What these kids are, in fact, doing is a much more significant kind of thinking than they have been asked to do by those who are testing them. They are – if you don't mind me being a little pretentious here – thinking in the great tradition of western thought. Plato, Augustine, Aquinas, Kant, Hegel, Marx, Freud would all agree with their priorities. This tradition says that logic (or reason) is never to be separated from what goes on in the real world and what should go on there, whether among human beings or in nature; our thinking is part of the process by which we help realize the potential of our world. Understanding reality and changing it always go hand in hand. Thinking always leads to action of one kind or another, even if it's a decision to do nothing. And action, in its turn, leads to more thought.

This tradition of thinking says, for example, that there are "concepts" in the world which are real things and through which we live our lives. These "concepts" hold our world together: capturing the contradictory particulars of nature and society (which we experience directly) and at the same time holding out the promise of their fuller development. "Concepts" express the tension between what's actual and what's potential. What is and what could be.

Such "concepts" are denied by our IQ testers and those who make up our fill-in-the-blanks exams.

Little kids, however, know what they are about. Take the concept of "mommy". Kids know very early that there are good mommies and bad mommies and that all mommies have good and bad qualities. This knowledge scares them. That's why stepmothers are such popular figures in fairy tales; a stepmother keeps the contradictory reality of mommy at a distance so that kids can deal with it more easily. Their own short histories also bring them a sense of the potential in mommy – what they can hope for in the future. Thus they develop a concept of "mommy" or "momminess" – that holds together their growing experience of "good" and "bad" mommies, through which they understand and act upon the world. What I want to stress here is that this involves tough thinking about what really goes on in their small but very intense society. Kids know their lives depend on it. They take it very seriously.

It is the same kind of thinking we saw with many of the kids who flunked our earlier IQ test. What they were being offered wasn't much of a challenge, but they did their best to make the questions real.

Let me say it again: Serious thinking involves figuring out our relations with nature and with each other.

When we deny the importance of this kind of thinking, which our ministries of education are now busily doing, we are stripping our kids of their deepest human heritage.

Nobody understands this better than working men and women, even if they often don't have the words to describe it. This understanding explains why workers have such disdain for what they call "ivory tower" thinking. They know that good thinking has to make a difference in the world, that it is deeply practical. "Really useful knowledge."

What workers and their kids rarely have – outside the field

of union and political action – is the opportunity to move back and forth from thought and action, to think actively over a long period of time. This is, of course, never permitted on the job. But in politics and in the union movement, where this is possible, that's where workers develop sophisticated thinking. That's where they become "smart." The potential is there; it just has to be used.

To put this another way, intelligence is not something fixed. It's fluid. It can be crushed; it can be created. There isn't a person in this room who hasn't experienced this in their own lives and in watching newcomers enter the union or some political battle. What an extraordinary thing it is to watch someone get smart or experience getting smart ourselves – in battling the boss or Brian Mulroney. And it happens every day in the labour movement and wherever resistance to oppression takes place. What we have to make certain is that it happens every day in school.

## *The Formal Program That Goes With Intelligence Labelling*

There is a whole informal or hidden curriculum in our schools, which I don't have time to discuss, but it's important to remember it's there. This is the social order of the school, which kids are expected to take as a "normal" social order: authority structures, how time is managed, how people speak to each other – that sort of thing. Kids resist it, but it cuts a lot of ice as the "norm" and undercuts thinking about an alternative social order.

The formal program, which I want to touch on here and which is the major public thrust of our ministries of education, fits hand in glove with the testing that I've been talking about.

It denies, for example, that we try to build "concepts" in our lives. It guts the social and scientific content of what kids learn in school. It focuses on such things as "thinking skills" in which content is irrelevant. It represses thought and language which have depth and strength of feeling. For our ministries of education anything goes by way of content – don't let the guidelines fool you – so long as the real world (its oppression and its joys) is avoided and the kids are kept in line.

There is nothing of "excellence" or "quality" here, the two major buzz words of the far right in education which our ministries now run with and which they have turned into the most complete public lies imaginable.

We have to be very clear about this: there are no serious purposes on our education ministries' agendas, other than the production of a docile workforce. For the different levels of the system they propose different levels of "Trivial Pursuit". It is what Frank Smith calls "programmed learning". Elementary "skills" for the bottom. Narrow high-tech "skills" for the top. No real learning for anyone. And everywhere the same process of putting words to words, filling in the blanks. What changes between the streams is the complexity of the classroom games, which in the end, of course, are deadly games, since they waste so much of our children's lives and determine so much of their future.

## *A Working Class Response*

I want to conclude with three points:

The first point is that working class kids resist the labelling, streaming and programming that comes down on them.

That's hardly news to the people in this room. But it's important to keep in mind.

Most working class kids resist the hidden curriculum of their schools in one way or another. As much as they can they cut out their own time and space within the school order – cutting up, cutting classes, avoiding work, dropping out.

And they resist the formal curriculum of the school – its thought and its language. They know this formal curriculum doesn't really get them anywhere. Its "qualifications" are largely irrelevant for most of the jobs seriously open to them. Its capacity to help them understand the world about them is nothing short of grotesque.

The problem with this resistance is that kids being kids, they throw out the intellectual and creative baby with the bath water of what passes for intellectual and creative work in school. If school work is what using your mind is all about, they say, we don't want to have anything to do with it. It is only when they get to be adults do they learn that what power and happiness they can hope for in life depends on their being able to use their minds.

In the course of this experience, most working class kids come to separate mental and manual labour, in one way or another, and end up "choosing" to do manual labour as the honourable and realistic choice. This fits perfectly with an identical split made in the capitalist workplace, where bosses do the thinking and workers carry it out. Workers may resist this split later on in their lives, but as school children they take it into their hearts.

The second point I want to make is that teachers resist this government/corporate thrust in education as well.

Most of this resistance is inarticulate, especially in public. It sounds strange to be saying this about teachers, who spend their days talking, but they – and here I'm thinking especially of their organizations – don't have many words to describe what they know is wrong about how our schools work and what should be done about it. Mostly teacher unions are focused on salaries and job security, like a lot of unions you know.

Individual teachers don't have a way of collectively dealing with their classroom concerns, of talking honestly about daily work problems with their fellow teachers or with parents in a safe environment. Their bosses do most of the public talking about what goes on and should go on within the school. As a result most teachers end up closing their classroom doors and working hard on their own to keep some order and program alive among their students. But in doing so they have little sense that things could really be different: that they don't have to be at war with their working class students and afraid of their communities; that they could have much more power than they do now over what happens to them at work; that their curriculum could be a lot more meaningful to both themselves and their students.

The recent government thrust in education, however, is

labelling, streaming and programming, which I touched on earlier, and which does more than hurt kids. It also hurts teachers, and much more obviously than in the past. Increasingly teachers are being treated more and more like workers. More and more they are being asked to take orders, not to think for themselves, to subject their classroom work to "teacher proof" programs and materials. Closing their doors doesn't work so well anymore.

Labour has to be there for teachers when they finally turn and fight over what should happen to kids in their classrooms, which they are now starting to do in places like British Columbia. In the end, kids' happiness and purpose in school are the teachers' happiness and purpose. Their interests are not opposed. This idea is hard to hold on to in the everyday practice of school politics and in the business unionism of so many of our teacher organizations. But it's true, and it's also true that most of the kids our teachers teach are working class kids. With enough good organizing we can all be on the same side.

My final point is that as Labour puts itself alongside student and teacher resistance in our schools, the key issue is what happens to kids in classrooms: the labelling, the streaming and the programming. It's all one package, part of one system. And that's how we have to deal with it.

We have to say what's wrong on all these fronts and we must also say what should take their place as part of a whole system.

We have to say "NO" to labelling working class kids – any kids at all – on the dumb/smart, crazy/sane spectrum. Don't tolerate it all. Sue the system for slander in the courts. And, more importantly, fight politically on every front there is to put a stop to it. None of these labels are necessary, even in today's bureaucratically controlled schools. There is a catholic school board in this province which hasn't given an IQ test since 1975.

We have to fight, instead, for classrooms where kids are defined as full citizens – members of a classroom community, capable of powerful and purposeful work. We do this not for any sentimental reason, but because that's the truth of the matter; the potential is there.

There are, of course, a very small number of kids who are honestly retarded or emotionally disturbed. They should be taken compassionately into the community of students and teachers; the last thing these kids need is to be thrown into lonely and humiliating ghettos, whether in special classes or special schools.

Of course, we need smaller classes to help make this kind of integration work and to give teachers the opportunity to make a deeper connection with all of their students. It's costly. But plugging a couple of corporate tax loopholes would do the trick. Seriously. There are billions of dollars available to the social sector even within our present tax structure.

We also have to say "NO" to any kind of streaming or placement that has a class, gender or racist bias – that is, a stream in which the people in it are somehow judged to be less than others: dumber or crazier. Not so able. Not so on top of their lives.

We have to fight, instead, for placement that insures a solid education for all our kids. Secretaries and plumbers, steelworkers and retail workers, mechanics and clerks must also be historians and economists, poets, intellectuals and artists. It is only through these activities that they can be full citizens. Many workers, of course, take on these tasks, but they are running deeply against the grain of what the society expects of them. We have to fight for placement which gives our kids access to all these activities.

In the end a serious curriculum means linking the work kids do in school with the larger fight to make a better world. It means telling the whole truth about the way things are and acting on that truth.

It will be a long and hard struggle. Mostly it will be kids of future generations who will benefit.

For the people in this room that comes as no surprise. The labour movement has had a proud history of lending a helping hand to the future – for freedom, for justice, for a life with love in it. We expect to continue doing this work. And if this conference is any indication, we know that nowhere is the future more at stake than in our kids' education.

The OFL has taken on a strong new mandate in looking out for working class kids in school. In so doing it has significantly changed the nature of the long battle this province's working people have had with their educational system. With union educators and activists like yourselves at the forefront of this battle, real victories on behalf of our kids are now possible. For all of those people – kids and adults – who have fought the good fight for working class kids in our schools, this is an important moment and one we should all be proud of.

*George Martell, a former school trustee on the Toronto Board of Education, teaches in the Social Science Department of Atkinson College, York University.*

# Chapter 3

## Keeping Workers In Their Place:
### The Role Of The Community College

*John Huot*

Each year I show my first year classes at Humber College a segment of the CBC series, "The Canadian Establishment", which aired originally about 10 years ago. The video describes how J.A. McDougald, the Canadian financier who controlled Argus Corporation until his death in 1978, dropped out of school at 14. "The worst mistake I ever made", he is quoted as saying, "I should have left when I was 12."

My students' chuckles trail off when they hear that the young drop-out travelled by limousine to his father's Bay Street stockbroker's firm, and after that to the top of the corporate elite in Canada. Meanwhile, thousands of working class dropouts of McDougald's generation ended up, if they were lucky, "on the line" of Argus-controlled companies such as Massey Ferguson or Dominion Stores.

This story illustrates the basic truth that your parents' socio-economic background, not your own ability or your educational qualifications, is the most important factor determining your "success" in the education system and in the job market. The role of the education system is not to develop students' ability and potential to the fullest. It is rather to serve as a sophisticated tool for the distribution of educational and job opportunities according to socio-economic background. It carries out this role by twisting and distorting the ability and potential of working class people to the requirements of employers.

## Education's Black Hole

Ontario's community colleges have an essential, though little understood, role in this system. I say "little understood" because the colleges seem to be a "black hole" between high school and university in the public consciousness. They are largely absent from media, public, and even political party policy debates about the education system. Employers have taken full advantage of this black hole in public awareness by seizing an overwhelming role in defining what and how college students learn. Colleges are the employers' "model" of the proper link between employers and schools, a model which they are now selling to high schools and universities.

For the labour movement and the majority of Ontario's working people over 18, community colleges have been the most important public education institution during the last 20 years. There are 22 colleges, located in every major and medium-sized city in the province, with about 200 satellite campuses in many smaller centres. They provide access to post-secondary education for about 100,000 full-time students (compared to about 170,000 university students) and non-post-secondary skills training to tens of thousands more students.

Community college graduates are much more likely than university graduates to work in unionized jobs, especially in the public sector, or in private sector jobs that are likely targets of future union organizing drives.

The community colleges' role in carrying forward for the over-18 population the streaming George Martell has described in elementary and secondary schools is also little known by the public. The opposition to the streaming role of elementary and secondary schools mounted by labour and community groups has been totally absent in the colleges. I'm referring, for example, to the Regent Park sole support mothers who exposed special education classes as tools for streaming their children into dead-end classes and jobs. I'm thinking also of the black parents who have exposed how their children are channelled into high school programs which rule out access to post-secondary education or to many skilled trades apprenticeships. And let's not forget how the Labour

Studies Liaison Committee of the Toronto Board of Education enabled union-appointed labour educators and sympathetic teachers to develop relevant learning materials for students on labour history and the realities of the world of work. I'm going to briefly describe how community colleges keep workers in their place by trying to answer three questions:
- Who goes to community college
- What do community college students learn?
- What happens to graduates in the world of work?

## Who Goes to Community College?

There are two large streams which lead students from secondary school to college:
- Non-Post-Secondary Programs, which do not require Grade 12 diploma
- Post-Secondary Programs, which require a minimum of Grade 12 diploma.

Non-post-Secondary Programs, representing 25-35% of the colleges' activities, draw on high school drop outs, Grade 12 graduates who do not pursue post-secondary programs, and immigrants. Programs include apprenticeships; technical skills courses a year or less in duration, and basic skills courses in English as a Second Language; job preparation for women, youth, etc. Non-post-Secondary students are overwhelmingly from "traditional" working class backgrounds. Few will go on to post secondary programs.

Many of these non-post-secondary programs have been cut back or phased out in recent years as a consequence of federal and provincial government policies to reduce skills training funding and to shift training funds to the private sector.

Post-Secondary Programs: The original mandate of the community colleges was to provide access to post-secondary education for sectors of Ontario's population which previously had little access: i.e. working people. Open door admissions to all Grade 12 graduates has been official provincial government policy since 1965, although additional entrance requirements have been allowed in most programs in recent years.

How open is the door? A 1983 survey showed that only

two in ten community college students were from the highest socio-economic group in Ontario, compared to five in 10 university students. The survey concluded that college students were more evenly spread across all socio-economic groups than university students. By this yardstick, working class students have significantly more access to colleges than universities.

Another yardstick of students' socio-economic background is their stream in secondary school. Most studies demonstrate that students in the three high school streams (Basic; General; Academic) come from the lowest to highest socio-economic groups respectively in Ontario. In recent years, an increasing proportion of successful college applicants is from the higher secondary school streams (Academic or General with some Academic-level credits), including an increasing proportion of Grade 13 graduates and of persons with some university. Only one in 10 General Level graduates (General credits only) goes to college, and only half of them will graduate. Grade 12 Basic Level graduates are formally barred from most post-secondary programs. Many colleges are abandoning the few programs to which these students have been previously admitted.

The community colleges' narrowing open door is also a revolving door for the approximately 45% of the students who drop out without completing their program. The lower the high school stream (and socio-economic background) of students, the more likely they are to drop out from college. Part of this is owing to academic disadvantages acquired in high school and part is owing to the financial crunch of working long hours in part-time jobs and carrying 20-30 hours a week in class/lab/field placement. Conclusion: the open door to access to post-secondary education at the colleges is narrowing for large segments of working class people in Ontario. A larger proportion of this group is now streamed directly into the workforce without the opportunity to pursue post-secondary studies.

## *What Do Community College Students Learn?*

Both Non-Post-Secondary and Post-Secondary students learn two things at college:

(1) They learn narrow, job-specific skills, whether hands-on technical skills or language and math skills. There is little emphasis on learning the principles of their disciplines as the foundation for further and more complex learning. There is even less emphasis on the realities of how their knowledge and skills are organized by employers in the world of work.

(2) Students also learn the virtues of loyalty, obedience, and conformity to established authority, to quote the OFL's recent brief to the Ontario Legislature's Select Committee on Education.

Within this broad framework of similar end results of learning at college, the two streams of students are treated differently in formal ways. Non-post-secondary students have no opportunity at all to access other than practical skills courses. Most union activists know from our experience in labour education programs the empowerment that results when workers learn together about their lives and work experience. I've seen this happen time and again when I taught labour history to unionists through a labour studies program my college co-sponsored with Metro Toronto Labour Council. The program was cancelled two years ago, partly because the senior administrators could not tolerate the independence of a union-controlled program which is routinely granted to employer-dominated programs. Perhaps more fundamentally, the community colleges simply have no commitment to educating workers beyond the hands-on skills training that keeps them "in their place".

Post-secondary students don't get much better. They also learn a narrow range of job-related knowledge and practical skills, with somewhat higher language and math-based skills if their future occupations require it.

In addition, post-secondary students are supposed to have one-third of their courses devoted to non-program/non-job related "general education". Over the years, this education component has been drastically reduced or diluted in most colleges, mainly through employer pressure to squeeze more job-related skill training into programs. Broadly speaking, the result is that English is taught not as a tool to understand and change students' life situation, but rather as a tool to be more useful to employers. For example, English courses focus on how to write business letters and job resumes. Even in the few colleges which still offer non-program-specific general education courses, it is extremely rare to find them rooted in students' real life experience with the goal of empowering them in the world of work and the community. The debate over the kind of curriculum and learning approaches that would meet the needs of students and the community, not employers, has found little place within the colleges. I believe the impetus for such a debate and for the changes we need will have to come from labour and community-based groups. That was certainly how these issues became public policy issues in the elementary and secondary schools.

## What Happens to Graduates in the World of Work?

The narrow knowledge and skills focus of most graduates gains them access to entry level jobs in their field. They discover they have little autonomy, responsibility, or upward mobility on the job. The narrow focus of their job functions, and of their college training, reflects the place of the colleges and their graduates in the larger division of labour and of the education system in society. During the last 30-40 years, employers and governments have sub-divided the job functions of many university-trained professionals such as engineers, architects,and social workers. More advanced technical knowledge and skills, as well as the skill of "managing" others' work, are learned in university; less advanced knowledge and skills, as well as the "skill" of working under the direction of superiors, are learned at college. Streaming in post-secondary education is obviously inspired by Taylor's scientific management principles!

Furthermore, it is almost as difficult to switch from a "lower" to a "higher" stream in the post-secondary system as it is in secondary schools. Ontario's community colleges, unlike Quebec's or B.C.'s, were set up as terminal, not transfer, post-secondary institutions. That means college graduates are not guaranteed admission to university, nor are they guaranteed any credit for their college courses.

## *Do Community Colleges Have a Future?*

This is a grim scenario I've painted. There's an even grimmer scenario, one I'm reminded of every day as I drive home past the shutdown Goodyear plant on Toronto's Lakeshore. The only workers there now are the wreckers. The plant is being dismantled department by department, floor by floor. Each day I go by, another section lies in rubble on the ground.

The community colleges face a similar fate. The colleges are being dismantled too – today it's program by program, campus by campus, perhaps tomorrow it will be college by college. After 20 years of priding themselves on their ability to train graduates in the specific shapes and sizes ordered by employers, to the point of abandoning most pretence to educating students, the colleges are being told by employers and governments that the private sector can train present and future workers better, quicker and cheaper.

It is significant that the first target of privatization is non-post-secondary programming, which has always had the mandate to provide skills training only, with no broader education. If indeed the community colleges are about job training only, why have colleges at all, if all they provide is a publicly-subsidized training service for employers? The answer is that our students and communities are entitled to more than the limiting and distorting of their abilities and potential currently offered by employer-dominated colleges or by employer-sponsored training. We have the right to expect that public education institutions will provide opportunities to learn both career-specific and social, cultural, and intellectual knowledge and skills, to empower learners in their lives at home, in their communities and in the world of work. Ontario's community col-

leges are currently undergoing their first comprehensive evaluation in 20 years by a government-appointed project called "Vision 2000". The employer, and government, agenda is clear:
(1) to make the colleges even cheaper, more effective tools for training loyal and obedient workers to employers's specifications;
(2) to downsize the colleges in terms of enrolment and educational opportunities and choices.
This agenda should be renamed Virus 2000.

Labour has a different vision of education in the year 2000, the vision we are articulating at this conference. That vision focusses on the right of all people, regardless of socio-economic, gender, racial/cultural, or (dis)ability background, to the full development of their talents in a publicly-funded, publicly-accountable education system. If that vision is to have any future in the community colleges, it is vital that Labour, including O.P.S.E.U., which represents the 16,000 teachers and support staff in the colleges, develop a broadly-based campaign for a community college which serves not to keep people in their place, but rather puts the educational needs of Ontario's working people and their communities in the first place.

*John Huot is a teacher at Seneca College and president of OPSEU Local 562.*

# Chapter 4

## *Equal Outcomes*
### *Penny Moss*

In this short presentation I am not going to identify the shortcomings of our present education system nor will I comment on the reasons for such shortcomings. But we do know that public satisfaction with the school system has been declining steadily, yet the public's expectation of what schools should be able to accomplish seems to grow, and I think rightly so.

Ronald Edmonds, a former Assistant Superintendent of New York schools wrote:

> We can, whenever we choose, successfully educate all children whose schooling is of interest to us. We already know more than we need, in order to do this. Whether we do it must finally depend on how we feel about the fact that we haven't done it so far...

It is clear to me that we do know enough; enough about child development, child psychology, about how children learn and the implications of this knowledge for teaching. But how do we feel about the fact that we have not educated students equally so far? Poor children and those whose parents work in semi-skilled or skilled occupations do less well in school than those whose parents are in professional fields. To many of us this is profoundly unjust; to others the schools are simply doing what they should - sorting students out for future occupations.

This sorting out is supported by Ministry of Education regulations and policies that direct young people to a secondary school system with three levels of difficulty: basic, general and advanced. There is a common belief that these levels provide for students' different levels of ability. In fact, students are sorted out at the end of Grade 8 on the basis of school success or lack of it. Therefore, we must focus our attention on what happens before Grade 8 as well as in secondary schools.

Ontario's stated policy is one of equal opportunity in education. It is time to shift our focus. There can be no equal opportunity unless there are equal outcomes. We have focused too much, I believe, on the differences between students in the name of respect for the individual. I think we need to focus on how students are the same.

Consider what all students have in common. First, with very few exceptions, they enter school at four of five years old having almost completely learned their first language. This is a staggering human accomplishment. They do it largely without the help of professionals and within their own homes. Children irrespective of their social class learn to speak and think, to make sense of their environment, to use talking and listening as ways of learning. Second, all parents, at least all of those that I have ever met, want their children to do well in school. Third, children, like adults, are social beings. They learn from and with each other as well as from adults. Relationships with teachers that foster confidence, and build trust and respect are important to the success of students. As well, parents and students need to know how well the student is doing in school.

We need schools that make these similarities in children the core of everything they do; where the learning of English or French – speaking, listening, reading and writing is central; where genuine partnerships with parents are built and where careful evaluation of student achievement and effective reporting to parents is routine.

However, a focus on what happens in individual classrooms is not enough. I believe that we need a major restructuring of the school system at the intermediate level - Grades 7-10.

## *A Common Curriculum To Grade 10*

Consider the schooling of 12-15 year-olds. At a time in their lives when they are most likely to be unsure of who they are or where they are going, they are often required to change schools twice, at Grade 6 and again at Grade 8. Friendships —so important to adolescents, are often interrupted and the student is faced with new subject disciplines, many more teachers, much larger institutions and a loss of parent connection to the school. Is it any wonder that the patterns of dropping out begin?

A more sensible arrangement would be to have kindergarten to Grade 6 in the familiar community schools followed by intermediate schools for Grade 7-10. Students would not be under a credit system. Instead they would receive a common curriculum in the areas of language, mathematics, science, arts, social studies, family studies and industrial arts, and a second language. In addition, they would experience the options available after Grade 10, for example, technical studies, business studies. They will have been taught for four years by a team of teachers that know them well and can provide real support and guidance in making choices for senior secondary schools.

Grades 11 and 12 and Ontario Academic Courses can be years of specialization where students can pursue their courses to university, college or work. This arrangement would make the development programs that link colleges and business and industry with schools in the interests of students more likely. But more importantly it would delay the making of decisions that affect the life chances of students until they reach the end of compulsory schooling.

It is time to organize schools in ways that make it possible for all students to learn more to learn well. We may then have a chance to come closer to achieving equality among students.

*Penny Moss, a former chair of the Toronto Board of Education, is currently the Executive Director of the Ontario School Boards Association.*

# Chapter 5

# Priorities For De-Streaming and For Improving Working Class Success

### Doug Little

When Jim Turk asked me to do a brief talk at this convention he said, "How can we do away with streaming and give working class kids a better deal in the education system?"

I had to think for a while about the perspective I would take. Would it be former school trustee, OISE student, magazine editor or classroom teacher? Together they form an eclectic pattern in my mind but seldom contradict each other. What I have come to learn in theory and in practice confirm and extend one another.

All of this business of anti-working class, anti-minority, anti-woman discrimination come together mainly under the heading of streaming. We have our work cut out for us if we ever want to seriously change things. Streaming by so-called "ability" seems to make a lot of sense to many members of the public. Most however don't realize how seriously it is skewed against workers and their kids.

When people find out that the basic and general streams are overwhelmingly composed of minority and working class students most begin to smell a rat. The comfortable, however, like it the way it is and will push back very hard against any real changes that threaten the established order.

I have come to believe that there are seven areas in which substantial gains can be made. These are in the areas of:

**1**. Organized parents
**2**. Appropriate curriculum

**3.** Appropriate pedagogy or teaching style
**4.** Teacher training and placement
**5.** Mainstreaming with care
**6.** Adult literacy
**7.** Sufficient staffing.

## *Parent Organizing*

Everything we know about unions applies directly to organizing parents. Trying to change school systems by yourself is impossible. As Pete Seeger tells us in *Talkin' Union*, "the boss won't listen if one guy squawks but he'd better listen if the union talks," applies just as well in parent organizing as in union organizing. Working parents should not go alone to parents meetings but should meet and talk first and then turn up at the first meeting with support. Otherwise you will be co-opted, out-voted and made to feel that your priorities are only your own. Most PTAs are middle class dominated with very limited agendas and are controlled by the local principal. In poor areas principals actually fear the sudden rising up of parent frustration and anger, especially in the housing projects. Eventually, if parents like these get organized, they must run candidates for the board of education.

There will be no real gains until the power of senior bureaucrats is broken and re-distributed to communities. It will require an organized political force to help accomplish this task. This is usually the NDP.

## *Appropriate Curriculum*

In order to have any interest in school (and by the way, most working class and minority kids act up because they are bored silly – weren't you?), kids must see themselves and the reality they know reflected in the school curriculum – its language, history, math, science, music, and so on.

Most textbooks have middle class situations with type-cast characters (remember Dick and Jane – father in a suit with a briefcase, mom at home baking pies.) They teach kids in school that you need to be a professional to be a success.

School curriculum only mirrors the biases of a class society. Row after row of Hardy Boys, Nancy Drew and Sweet Valley High. All totally middle class, white and outside the experience of the kids we want to help – a complete reversal of the proportions in society. Only a few books by S.E. Hinton, Frank Bonham and Gloria Miklowitz are based on working class and minority characters. These books are loved by our kids and more need to be written to keep them reading.

When it comes to history, once again our kids fail to see themselves and their reality. Events are Eurocentric, out of context in world history, racist, classist and sexist mainly by omission but also by stereotype.

It doesn't have to be that way. To take one possible approach, consider starting kids out by looking at films like *Spartacus*, *Cry Freedom*, *Robin Hood*, *Roots*, *Gandhi* and *Norma Rae*. In films like these we have a context for history. Kids can see what the important elements of history really are.

They can see, for example, that in the ancient world of Spartacus, people from many different cultures were slaves. It is especially important for black children to know that their ancestors were not the only slaves in history. From *Robin Hood*, kids can examine the feudal system to note that slaves had become serfs and slave owners had become landlords. When we move to *Norma Rae*, they can see that in the modern world there are still haves and have-nots in relation to power and wealth. In this context, they come to understand that throughout history there has always been a minority with most of the power and wealth in the society and a restless majority kept in line by soldiers and politics.

The stories behind *Roots*, *Gandhi* and *Cry Freedom* show that there is an international dimension to this struggle. Kids learn imperialism and colonialism along with slavery, feudalism and capitalism.

With this history behind them, kids have a context for the rebellions of 1837, Louis Riel, the building of the CPR – the grist for the grade eight history mill.

Even in math the study of percentages this past week in my classroom took on a new meaning when the class discovered that women make 66% of what men make and that 5% of

Canadians own 48% of all the wealth. Do you see what I mean!

## *Appropriate Pedagogy*

Working class kids and minority kids have a great deal of difficulty sitting in rows doing mindless seatwork over and over all day. They rebel against it and get themselves into trouble. Everything we know about education tells us that this is not how children learn. When we think back ourselves to the important things we have learned in our trade it was usually done co-operatively in a small group using mainly a hands-on method.

There is a growing body of literature concerning active-learning and co-operative learning in schools which we must embrace and fight for if our democratic curriculum proposals are to match our teaching practice.

Kids need to be grouped in units of four or five and mixed by race, gender and ability to learn. This not only creates the best learning environment because we soon discover that the "best" students do not always have the "best" ideas but students learn to co-operative more than they compete. Ultimately, this should help break down racial, gender barriers and even reduce tension in our society. Perhaps even help put an end to war.

## *Teacher Training and Placement*

Most teachers were not trained in active learning and co-operative learning and resist it as much as possible. There must be a great deal more professional development to facilitate this shift.

Three quarters of the teachers in our "inner city" schools don't want to be there. Some are obliged to stay because of subject specialties, like French. Others stick around because they are burnt out and are waiting for retirement in familiar circumstances. Still others are careerists who need the adminsitrative experience these schools can offer them – as chairpersons, vice-principals, and principals – to move up the bureaucratic ladder.

Those who remain, often four or five political lefties of one kind or another, are there for good reasons. This is where they think they are supposed to be if they are to make a difference for poor working class kids.

Four or five committed teachers are not good enough staffing for a priority inner city school.

Boards need incentive to attract quality teachers into inner city schools.

At a recent voluntary service transfer (VST) meeting in North York, teachers had a chance to really size up the response of their colleagues to the tensions of inner city teaching. (VST means "get me out of that school and place me. I'll go anywhere.") Before administrators could take hold of the meeting one teacher asked how many were fleeing from west of Yonge (the working class and inner city district). Eighty hands shot up. She then asked how many wanted out of an east end school (the middle class area). One hand slowly crept up. This is the situation: it is hard to get anyone to teach in inner city schools, let alone get enough high-quality teachers.

There are immediate ways to help. Smaller classes; more day-to-day democracy; serious curriculum development controlled by the teachers; great libraries; school-community organizers; generous supplies and audio-visual equipment; more support staffing among secretaries and caretakers – all these things make a difference in attracting teachers and making things better for the kids. The two go hand in hand.

## *Mainstreaming*

It is now an article of faith that the progressive community supports mainstreaming: that is to say placing students in the least restricted environment (usually the regular class) in which the child can function. When the Toronto Star and the Liberals start to support it you know its overdue. Some boards support the concept only because it is cheaper. The savings from returning kids to the regular class are, however, rarely spent on the regular class. And returning some students to a large regular class, other things being equal, is no solution; new, equally unjust, streams will emerge.

Something much more fundamental has to change in the schools if we are to effectively integrate working class students. It will involve much more serious changes in curriculum, in pedagogy – all the things we have learned about team teaching, for example – and in school administration.

There are, of course, some deeply disturbed kids, who need more support than any regular class can offer. We don't gain when they are mainstreamed – the whole class suffers – but at the same time they ought not to be ghettoized in institutions. Much more human support is required within the neighbourhood school framework to provide a way back to the regular classroom.

## *Adult Literacy*

We must be very careful here not to give the system an out and let adult literacy become a blame-the-victim-solution. We must, however, acknowledge the most common characteristic of poorly educated children is that they are the sons and daughters of poorly educated parents, especially poorly educated single mothers. Twenty percent of our adult population have less than grade eight education. Their children make up a considerably greater percentage of our school population.

We need then to make a dramatic effort to raise the literacy level of those who are "functionally illiterate" and have children in school. They must become the target group for school board literacy efforts. The OFL is to be congratulated for its literacy efforts in recent years. They must not, however, be the only players in the field. Community-based literacy and school board literacy must be beefed up.

Literacy is not just reading words, it is understanding the world around us at the same time. Adult literacy classes of all types must be used to help people understand power relationships of class, race and gender so that the newly literate will be empowered to change the world around them.

## *Sufficient Staffing*

Usually the curriculum and pedagogy people show disdain towards those who still say smaller classes are the answer. It is not the answer but it is an answer.

My Grade 8 class is typical of those in a poor urban setting. It has only 22 kids – a dream number only a few years ago. In this class mainstreaming means something quite different than in middle class areas, where it might involve one or two Special Ed kids per class. It now includes seven Special Education students including three "behavioural" students and one retarded student reading at the grade one level. Only five of these students are to be placed in high school next year in an entirely Advanced stream. Three more will have a mixed General/Advanced timetable. Of the entire student body in Ontario, 55% are in Advanced programs but only 24% of this class will be.

I can seldom stay long enough or get around often enough to help all the kids who need help.

I have not the slightest hesitation in proposing that these types of classes be capped at 15 students and if improvement in result is not seen soon then cut again. This would mean only 20 to 30 teachers in a large board like North York at a cost of about $1.5 million. For Metro as a whole the cost would be about $6 million. Extra teachers seem to be made available for middle class priorities but not for the poor.

We all know that every cent that is not spent on inner city education will not be saved but will eventually be spent anyway. The only difference is that it will be spent on police, courts and jails.

Thank you very much for your attention to this list of priorities for the reform of education. I can only hope that the labour movement will get behind these issues in a solid fashion. If not now then when? If not labour then who?

*Doug Little, a former school trustee on the Toronto Board of Education, now teaches at Lawrence Heights Middle School in North York.*

# Chapter 6

## Changing Education Through Politics: Labour and the NDP

*Richard Johnston*

I was raised north of Peterborough in a place called Dummer Township, and I do not kid you about that. It was settled in 1827, and in 1964 I was the first person ever to go to university from that township. It was not that it was aptly named, it was that the residents were subsistence farmers; basically, they farmed rocks.

At any rate, they were poor farmers and, like the working classes in the cities, they were generally left to their own devices. A lot of structures were put in place to make sure they stayed where they were and did not get the kind of education that the middle class accepts and expects.

I want to talk about organizing and where we go from here. This conference is the first step – a step that I actually would not have imagined was possible a few years ago – where unionists come together to talk about education in the larger sense and not just about trade union education that has been the focus for many, many years. This is a very historic moment that most of society doesn't realize has happened, but the revolution is beginning today, and you should know that you're here for it.

## Representing Labour and the NDP

Let's talk first about neighbourhoods. I agree with what Doug Little says about the need to get to parents and to involve them in making changes in the education system. And I want to underline his point of collective action. It is very dangerous for us to think that the way to get involved is as individual parents – to go out and get active in our home and school association and presume that that is going to do anything. In Scarborough they hardly exist at all – and those that do exist have their own neat little hierarchy: a small group of middle class and upper-middle class people who control what goes on. One person coming in as ginger would very quickly be put aside and made fairly useless.

Instead, we have to think about working from a base of strength. This should take place first with the people you work with, trying to get them to understand the issues that have been raised here about why the education system has failed them, why it is likely to fail their kids as well, and why they should get involved. From there, trade unionists should urge their local bargaining unit, and then their union, to be more active on education issues in the communities.

There are several other platforms and places where you can also have an effect.

One is your local NDP riding association. I would say that in the 1970's, as a party, we were very, very active in education issues and in developing a number of progressive policies. Unfortunately, we have slipped from that. In the last decade we have largely ignored education. We have forgotten that it is a dangerous institution that preserves the status quo, holding down people and their politicization. We've done so at our peril.

It is very important for you as a person who lives in a specific riding to be involved with the party locally. Let me give you the example of Scarborough West. Maybe you're a CAW worker at the General Motors van plant in the riding. You should go to your local union executive and talk about your need to have representation on the local NDP executive. You should argue for representation on a number of grounds, not just for the straight labour connection, but also around the issue of education. Most riding associations can easily develop a small sub-committee on education where the local unions from that area could be active members and start to play a role.

If you want to seriously affect your local board or your

local school, it's a lot easier for you to go before that institution representing, for example, Local 303, saying: "Here I am; we have 2700 workers in our plant, and we believe this about education. We don't like what's happening, for instance, with the streaming policies of the Scarborough Board of Education, and we want to hear you state today that you will initiate a totally de-streamed high school in the area where we have most of our workers. We will support you in doing that." You can then come in another door of the same meeting of that board as a representative of the local Scarborough West NDP association saying the same kind of thing but from a different perspective. But going in as an individual will get you no respect.

All the principles of solidarity that we use when we do trade union organizing in general should be used when we think about trying to organize around educational issues in our local community.

Our goals must certainly include getting parents in charge of their schools. This is a really important point. It is a highly subversive point. But first you have to get people politicized before you try organizing for parent power. Otherwise, you will just have local community councils, in the hands of the usual elite and not affected by the ideas that we are talking about here today.

## *The NDP Policy Review*

Let me talk a little bit about the NDP policy review and how I would love people like you to participate. In just a few weeks time, we will be sending a letter to every member of the NDP across the province saying that we want them to participate in the review of our policy for our next convention, probably in the fall of 1990. We will say we would like you to get involved in a number of ways. We want you to participate in a newsletter so that we can exchange ideas during the next number of months. We would also like you to do some work within your local riding association to make sure there is an educational subcommittee to deal with our policy review. I hope, as well, that you will work with your local unions to make sure that they are represented on these subcommittees so that we will have a good class analysis for our education policy as it comes forward in 1990.

I would like you to help us organize, out of my office, regional conferences across the province of Ontario where people who are New Democrats, labour activists, and members of the teaching federations will come together and discuss a series of issues. Through these conferences I hope we will develop resolutions that can go back to riding associations for their response, to then be sent off to our convention in the form of motions. If this happens, for the first time in a long time, it would be the grassroots who have a major say in the development of policy and not some critic who happens to have his own biases and opinions. The Caucus knows we can't always lead from the front, but should also be working behind the membership and getting them to make the changes that are necessary.

The role that I can see for you all, and I would actually implore you to play, would be to be available to us as people who would participate in those regional meetings, who would get other people out of your plants and offices to come to those meetings. We have a number of challenges and contradictions in our policy that really have to be confronted. We have a number of major issues that by the next election have to be in focus or they are going to be lost to us as issues for a long, long time.

## *The Liberals' Agenda*

This brings me to a discussion of the Ontario Liberal government's agenda at the moment. The Liberals understand that for them to have credibility as a reformist party, they have to be seen as reformers in education. That's why during the last election they came through with a smaller class size solution. They had not thought it through; they hadn't worked out its problems; they didn't understand the incoherence of lowering class sizes in Grades 1 and 2 while forgetting Grade 3 and kindergarten as parts of the primary division. They hadn't worked out any of these things or the effect their proposal would have on teacher shortages.

But they knew that, symbolically, the class size legislation was important. They knew that out there everyone understood that class sizes were too big and that their own children were not getting the kind of assistance they should be getting. The NDP was not positioned at all to respond to this initiative in terms of the quality of education, let alone provide any analysis about what was involved in it. We cannot have that happen again.

The issue of streaming is the most crucial structural issue we have to deal with. We are in danger of this issue being liberalized in a way that will mean that real de-streaming will never take place. The Liberals are clearly moving in this direction, especially following their troubles over the last couple of months with auto insurance and a number of other things, which have taken the bloom off the Peterson government. Education emerged again to refurbish the government's reformist image. Their first move was to offer early kindergarten opportunities for all children in the society. This initiative, it turned out, was really to find a cheap way to provide day-care. The other thing they decided to do was to move on de-streaming, but what they've announced is in my view a very frightening approach to the question.

All the government has done is to suggest that de-streaming be moved to the end of Grade 9 from the end of Grade 8. They are not putting in any extra assistance at all. There are not going to be smaller class sizes. There will be no retraining of high school teachers to allow them to deal with heterogeneous classes. There will not be the kinds of adjustments that are necessary if you are going to actually make it work. I think they are setting it up as a clear failure that will mean that de-streaming will die in the future. If we allow de-streaming to be dealt with only on the basis of easing the transition of kids from Grade 8 to Grade 9, and do not see it as a remedy for the larger structural problem that has been used to hold back kids from the working classes for generations, we will never get a chance to restructure the system.

This is a really important moment for Ontario New

Democrats to get their act together around the de-streaming issue. We have fairly good policy on it at the moment, but we really need to have it reinforced and refined in co-operation with the labour movement. If we do not do it in a very solid way, we are going to run into problems. In the next election we can be left again with nothing to say that will distinguish us as reformers in the education process.

## A Voice For Labour And Teachers

On another subject, this fall the Ontario Legislature's Select Committee on Education is going to be meeting on the financing of education. We cannot afford to go through fall hearings this year, as we did last year, with the only major labour representation being made by the Ontario Federation of Labour. This was one of the best performances we have had before us without any doubt, but we heard from nobody else. Now is the time for you to go back to your own unions and say to them that it is important to have the labour movement represented at those fall hearings. When you talk about financing of education you can talk about anything you want in education, because questions of finance provide the underpinnings for everything else. It's very important for people to start organizing now so that by September they will be in a position to make presentations to the Committee. The longer we have the union movement staying away from those kinds of hearings and letting the Canadian Federation of Independent Business and the chambers of commerce push their values on us, then the longer the disequilibrium of the system will continue. So I encourage you to take that on as a challenge in the next little while.

It is also crucial that we link our work with progressive forces in the teachers' federations. Teachers have real problems knowing whether they want to be unionists or professionals. They often see these things as contradictory. I have never understood why they have to be contradictory at all. It is a status thing, I guess. The Ontario Teachers' Federation, unlike the Ontario Federation of Labour, has so many problems of solidarity that it is a wonder that it is able to continue to exist at all. Its member federations are very much at each others' throats for jurisdictional reasons, which makes concerted political action very difficult. The only unifying factor I can see at the moment is the Ontario government trying to take away their pensions.

Other than that, on almost every other issue you can imagine, there are problems. Not the least of these problems is the fact that teachers do not necessarily all see themselves as progressive forces in education. They are very conscious of changes being imposed on them all the time without their professional input and experience, particularly over the last 25 years. Many have developed the attitude that they do not want change at all, often because they do not think they are ever really going to get their say in it or get it done in a way that respects their experience.

Until the recent initiatives of the OFL there hasn't been much dialogue around education issues between teacher federations and the union movement. It is crucial this dialogue begins expanding on all fronts. Within those federations are an awful lot of progressive people, an awful lot of people who need some bolstering if they are going to face change and if they are going to promote change. And they find it difficult, frankly, within their own structures, to do so.

So, I would encourage you again to think about tactics and ways, at the local level, as well as at a regional and provincial level. Your locals can have contacts with the Ontario Public School Teachers' Federation or the Federation of Women's Teachers' Associations of Ontario or the Ontario English Catholic Teachers' Association or the Ontario Secondary School Teachers' Federation or the Association des enseignants et des enseignantes franco-ontariens and develop some real connections.

## *The NDP And Teacher-Labour Dialogue*

The NDP will be going into our next convention with the hope that we can come up with a coherent policy that will reflect the kind of philosophical attitude that's been talked about today. We have a real problem in having five major affiliates of the

Ontario Teachers' Federation who for various reasons will be opposed to different aspects of what we want to do. It is really important as we move into a dialogue with teachers next January and February at our regional meetings, that they do not come to those meetings in a defensive posture, fighting for the historical positions of vested interest taken by their associations, afraid of change in particular areas and of the competition around change with other federations. It is important that they come looking at things from a fundamental perspective – that they are open to a major review of where education should be going and what schools should be.

The best technique for fostering that kind of view is to bring teacher affiliates – at local, regional, and provincial levels – in close contact with individual union leaders at the local level and with labour councils in their regions. They especially need discussions about the philosophical basis of equality of education that we are talking about here today. If we don't want our education policy process to explode at us at our convention, if we want it to move towards a consensus, it is really important for teachers and labour to get involved in that sort of process.

This is a very important moment for all of us involved in education. We cannot afford to lose it. We must not get caught up in just the issues themselves, even though they are vitally important. We must take some organizational first steps, if today's conference is to be more than a once-in-a-lifetime event that never went anywhere. We must make certain it is the first step to major change.

*Richard Johnston is the MPP for Scarborough West and the NDP's education critic in the Ontario Legislature.*

# Chapter 7

# High Tech Skills:

## The Corporate Assault On The Hearts And Minds of Union Workers

*Doug Noble*

## Introduction

It is a privilege to be here on what is really an historic occasion.

I want to provide a broad picture of one aspect of training, education and skills that is often overlooked.

I am hoping that my remarks are not premature to a Canadian audience. Even though you might not have experienced some of the things I will discuss this morning as much as American workers have, there is no doubt the Canadian labour movement is far more progressive than its American counterpart. Where I come from, the letters NDP still stand for "not dressed properly" or maybe "no demonstrations please."

Preparing this talk has given me the chance to explore a puzzling question that I've been carrying around in my gut for a number of years. As Gord Wilson suggested yesterday, I've been trying to listen to my gut, to follow my instincts on this question, in order to try to understand what's really going on.

The questions is this: why, in an increasingly high-tech work world that displaces or de-skills more and more workers every week, do corporate pronouncements endlessly promote sophisticated education and training as the key to corporate competitiveness and worker survival?

What do they mean by this? What do they really want? What

is their agenda? What do they mean when they tell us that we need all kinds of new sophisticated skills in order to survive in the new world of the "information age"?

Steel plants and auto plants and all sorts of other manufacturing plants are closing in the U.S. every month. Huge numbers of workers are laid off from their jobs due to new technological decisions. Workers' crafts and lifetime skills are eroded by new technological systems that require fewer and fewer of such master tradesmen and women. How can anyone say, with all this, that workers need even more sophisticated skills than ever before?

I want to warn you ahead of time that I'm going to be speaking about the down side, the underside of training this morning – what's bad about it. Of course, the opportunity to train and to learn throughout one's life can be hugely rewarding for one's personal growth and dignity, for one's job security and advancement, for one's understanding of the world, and for an expansion of one's role as an actor within it.

Those of you here who work with BEST and with all the other trade union training and education programs in Ontario are keenly aware of how valuable your programs can be for those you are helping.

As my mother always told me: "Douglas, learn, learn, they can't take that away from you."

What, after all, could be wrong or bad about training, learning, knowledge? Yesterday we discussed a lot of what's wrong with what passes for education in our schools. Today, as I speak with you, my 16-year-old daughter is crammed in a huge stuffy room with hundreds of other 16 year-olds taking her SATs – the ridiculous, biased, standardized exams that measure her supposed learning and go a long way to determine her future. I called her last night and we agreed to be thinking of each other this morning. So I just want to say, "good luck Rebecca"!

Such tests as she is taking are indicative of a lot that is wrong with an education system that functions against kids.

Today I want to talk about what's wrong with the kinds of training and learning that work against workers. I want to suggest that training and learning are not always a good thing and that knowledge is not always power.

## *Future Shock: Setting Us Up*

As a backdrop to our discussion, we have to understand first of all that we have all been subject to a massive, unrelenting propaganda campaign for at least a decade now. It has been telling us that the future will be altogether different from the past; that we are entering something called the information age, a computer age, an age of global competitiveness that will be unlike anything we have ever experienced before.

One example of this message is the copy of a life insurance advertisement. It reads, "the speed of light is 186,281 miles per second, but that's nothing compared to the speed the future is coming at you." The consequences of this endless corporate battering is that we begin to believe it.

Many of us have begun to wonder about our own experiences, our own skills, our own expertise. Will we be prepared for what is to come? Are we sufficiently computer-literate? Savvy about the new technologies? Do we understand the new production processes, the new statistical quality control methods? Are we ready or able to learn all the new things we will have to learn in order to keep our jobs, to advance in our jobs, to get other jobs? At least as important, or even more so, will our children be prepared for the brave new workplace ahead?

For most of us, there is something profoundly unsettling about this supposed new world we are entering. This puts us at a disadvantage because we find ourselves on the defensive when we talk about training and learning new skills. We feel, to a greater or lesser extent, that our own resources, our own wealth of experience on the job, our own hard-won crafts and mastery and workmanship, our own lifetimes of experiences will be no more help for what is to come.

As if to reinforce this message, to drive another nail in the coffin of our cherished past experience, a recent Congressional report of the Office of Technology Assessment in the United States entitled, "Technology and the American Economic Transition," concludes with the ominous words: "You can't go home again."

## *Why Sophisticated Skills?*

So, let me return to my original question. Over the last few years, corporate management and their propagandists have been telling us that training and education and new skills are now the key to the American and Canadian economic competitiveness.

For example, the new Canadian report of the Advisory Council on Adjustment (the de Grandpré Report) the corporatist guideline for Canadian citizens adjusting to the Free Trade Agreement, says that a skilled workforce "is a key, if not the key, to competitiveness and growth." Not surprisingly the Council's recommendation regarding the continuing education and training of Canadians constitutes, for them, the very core of the report.

In the U.S., too, the Congress Office of Technology Assessment report mentioned earlier contends that "the key ingredient in the new information society is a productive system for teaching and learning." A well-trained, highly skilled, sophisticated, knowledgeable, flexible, intelligent, adaptable, creative workforce, we are told again and again, is the key to competitiveness in a global high tech economy.

One result of this pronouncement, in the U.S., is that schools across the country have been stiffening their graduation requirements: more math, more science, more computers, more problem-solving exercises, more reasoning skills. No time for art, no time for music, no time for recreation, no time for hellraising. "Kids, you will need all you can fill your heads up with to make it in tomorrow's high tech world." So the story goes.

But, wait. All I know from today's world tells me that work on every level is being deskilled and workers displaced by the introduction of new technologies.

Secretaries have automatic spell-checkers and grammar checkers. Most workers' computation is done automatically by computer. Skilled machinists are slowly being replaced by less skilled and lower paid operatives of CNC machines or, at least, there are fewer machinists in the plant (and if CAD/CAM ever works there will be none).

Teachers' skills are replaced by packaged curricular and foolproof "effective" teaching methods or by computer-aided instruction (to give those kids that "individual" attention.)

An audiologist friend of mine tells me that now they have a machine that will measure all the variables of a person's hearing loss and burn a customized chip for a customized hearing aid automatically. So much for her job.

Meanwhile, modular construction methods threaten construction trades; self-diagnostic technologies practically fix themselves; and modular electronic components in cars can be replaced by a novice, threatening the skills and jobs of service technicians of many stripes. Even dentists fear that new dental preventive technologies will make them obsolete. And, yes, there is a bright spot in all of this. Middle managers are also threatened with obsolescence by computer management and telecommunication systems.

So, with all of this deskilling and displacement, what is all this talk of the new sophisticated skills, new sophisticated training for the hightech workplace?

Will we all become engineers? Programmers? Systems designers? Robotics experts? Sorry. Although the propaganda tells us that these are fast growing areas – the fastest growing areas in the job market – it neglects to tell us how few of these jobs there are and will be. If you start with one robotics expert and then you have five, you've got a 400% increase. A fast growing field, but you still only have five jobs. Even programmers, by the way, are threatened with obsolescence as automated software development is developed in the future. Ironically, programmers are contributing to their own obsolescence. Some people are less aware than others.

The real growth area in jobs, if you haven't heard by now, is in the low paying end of the service sector. Nurses aides, janitors, security people, food service. So what, again, is all this talk about sophisticated skills? By now I hope that you see why I've been so puzzled.

### *"Computer Literacy": A First Job*

In order to begin to unravel the mystery, I'd like to discuss one prime example of this corporate rhetoric. This is one that I have investigated pretty carefully for a number of years: the push for "computer literacy." This was the rage in the U.S. for a long time and in Canada as well.

Overnight, it seemed, about six or seven years ago, the entire population was informed that in order to function in society we would all have to know about computers. How to use them. How to program them. How they work.

In response, again, almost overnight in the U.S., computer literacy became the required subject in schools across the nation from elementary schools to high schools. And blue ribbon panels began to call computer literacy a new "basic skill," up there with the three R's. Want ads, too, suddenly began to include the phrase "computer literacy a must" for new jobs. It is no surprise that people began lining up for training courses in computer literacy and those who hesitated for whatever reason were labelled "computerphobic." They were seen as fearful, in need of psychological help. AT&T addressed this issue in an ad headed, "To Cure Technophobia You Need A Good Psychologist."

Back then it certainly appeared obvious that training in computers was the key to unlock the new world sculpted on a silicon chip, the St. Christopher's medal that would protect us and keep us from being left behind.

So what happened? In this mad rush, many thousands of people became comfortable with the new machines. They felt okay having them around. But, meanwhile, a large number began to discover that their new computer literacy wouldn't really get them a job as a programmer or systems analyst. At best it would get them a job typing on a word processor or as a data entry clerk. People found that knowing a little about computers was not really much of a help, was not much of a skill, at all.

Little did they realize however, that the push for computer literacy had accomplished precisely what its promoters had set out to do. This was three things: first and foremost, it was to scare people into sitting down in front of those screens so that they would get used to having those computers around. The point was to get people friendly with the technology. Just as computers were being made user-friendly, people had to be made computer-friendly. Take a look at the graphics from a manufacturing journal and you'll see a nice little picture: "Let's shake hands; let's welcome the new technology."

The second thing on the computer literacy campaign agenda was to deluge the schools and the homes and the offices and the factories with computers, without generating resistance.

The third was to distract people, to get them so bewildered, so involved in learning and thinking about computers, that they would not have time to think about other things, like: what justified the purchase of all those millions of computers? how would having all those computers around change their lives for the worse? why were they never a part of the decision-making process that was deciding the shape of their futures? Or, are Canadian and Japanese people really in competition with each other? Or, is it some huge multinational scam to bewilder us? What is all this talk about global competitiveness?

One result of the blitzkrieg campaign of computer literacy is that the United States schools have now spent over $2 trillion on over 1.5 million computers. In Ontario, the numbers are 85,000 computers at a cost of almost $1.5 billion in an eight year period. And there is still negligible research showing what good they're for. So people are scurrying around trying to figure out what to do with them.

I am currently involved in a project evaluating the Ontario Ministry of Education massive expenditures on computers in schools. I can tell you that a report just out from the Ontario Provincial Auditor finds negligible justification for the huge expense for Ontario's development of the ICON educational computers in schools. I do not know how many of you are aware that

Ontario developed its own computer hardware and software - the only project like it in North America. One purpose of that ICON was to promote Ontario computer manufacturing industry locally. I have to tell you that all the ICONs now used are made exclusively in Korea.

One footnote to the story about computer literacy. I had the rare opportunity to speak to a key government figure in the States, a man, with close links to industry, who put the computer literacy campaign together. During a conversation about an entirely different matter, he volunteered the information, with an arrogant, smug, proud, self-congratulatory smile, that he and his corporate cronies had invented the computer literacy campaign as a cover, a smokescreen, to get people sufficiently confused so that he and his friends could bring all those computers into the schools. He was proud of it. I must tell you that rarely does a writer's suspicions meet with such blatant confirmation.

## *Assaulting The Hearts Of Workers: Distraction and Compliance*

So what does this example of computer literacy have to do with what I want to talk about today? I think it serves as a cautionary tale — a warning that training and new skills are not always what they appear to be.

It warns us to be aware of new so-called literacies or numeracies (that's a new word), new-fangled know-how we are being asked to learn without a clear sense of the implications for ourselves individually and, more importantly, collectively.

This example also offers us the first answer to the puzzle: why corporations are pushing our needs for new training and skills. The answer is in part that this push is a smokescreen, a con game designed to destabilize us, to distract us, to get us concentrating real hard on the wrong things so we don't try to understand what is really going on. It is a way also of making us feel uncomfortable enough with our present skills so that we scramble to become comfortable with the new technologies, which allows their introduction without resistance. Finally, it is a way of getting us to blame ourselves for being locked out of opportunities in jobs and job advancements that were never really available to us anyway. It makes us accept that it's our fault because we lack the sophisticated skills. This example also gives us two reasons why corporate propagandists call such minimal skills as computer literacy "sophisticated skills."

First, their sophistication is what rubs off on a worker when he or she works with a sophisticated piece of technology. One acute scholar once noted how the term "semi-skilled" was invented around the 1830s by the stroke of a pen. What happened was that the head of the census bureau decided that anyone working all day with machinery would henceforth no longer be called unskilled; he or she would have a new rating – semi-skilled. In a flash, the minimal skills of machine tender became more sophisticated than those of a farmer who had mastered a lifetime of running a farm.

Another example of this: I was once visiting the head offices of a Rochester supermarket chain a few years ago and the personnel director tried to explain to me that a cashier running food over a laser scanner had more sophisticated skills than the traditional cashier. Somehow the sophistication of the laser lent sophistication to the job.

When I was a kid, I was a bagboy all through high school. I was scared to death to run one of those cash registers, I never thought I would be able to do it. Now, they say, that really was not anything, that it was not a sophisticated skill compared to running those cereal boxes and those milk cartons over that scanner.

Another reason it is more "sophisticated," I might say, is now you've got to do two jobs. You got to do this, and you got to bag. In the U.S., you've got to ask the customer, "you want a a paper bag or you want a plastic bag?" Pretty sophisticated skills. It's also clear by now that people working with computers, too, are portrayed as having more sophisticated skills than those who do not. So that is one meaning of sophisticated.

A second meaning of "sophisticated," illustrated by computer literacy, has to do with the right attitudes on the job. A person who learns something about computers displays a willingness to improve him or herself, a commitment to the company's technological investment, an eagerness to do the right thing, to adapt, to fit in.

Here "sophisticated" means having class, which in corporate terms, means acting professionally, acting like a manager, for the good of the company and for the good of one's own career. No wonder the recent Canadian Advisory Council On Adjustment to the Free Trade Agreement, in emphasizing new needed skills, speaks above all about the need to change attitudes toward the technology, toward what's good for the company, toward what's good for oneself as an individual. This is the real adjustment expected of new age workers. Now it's called a "skill."

One management consultant cited "an ability and willingness to take individual responsibility for the production process" as the most important factory worker skill required by the new computer telecommunications technology. Such responsible behavior, above all, is cited as the reason behind employers' increasing the pay rate of some jobs, even though other skill requirements are reduced.

The same consultant I mentioned points out that sophisticated new workers are also those who are willing to do any task, who are willing "to part with work rules that can constrain the range of work an individual can do." That is, they are willing to give away the fruits of years of union struggle in an instant. How can they do this? Because, according to this management analysis, workers with "mature", sophisticated skills are those who "trust their employers."

The U.S. Department of Labor recently issued a report called "Workplace Basics – Skills Employers Want," which tells us that "a new kind of American worker is being ordered up." And what are the skills of this new kind of worker? Above all, according to the Department of Labour, the worker must have "personal management skills", the ability to "maintain self-esteem," to set goals, to be motivated. Workers must be capable of taking charge of their own working lives, must be willing to change tasks at a job, to be retrained, to change jobs again and again in their lifetime. And they must be willing to accept a new more temporary arrangement with their employers in which a company's commitment to its workers is severely reduced. According to the report, the new worker "must be responsible for himself or herself for his or her own career development and job security."

So "sophisticated" here means two forms of high class professional style. It means being responsible to the company – showing effort, commitment, motivation, obedience, while expecting nothing in return from employers. And secondly, it means being responsible for oneself. A self-manager. An entrepreneur. Manage your time and manage your career and manage your goals. Sort of a freelancer who is not dependent on the employer for job security, for advancement, for benefits. Someone who has the class to give all to a company yet who also has the class to land on his or her feet with a smile when the employer no longer needs his or her services – with no hard feelings.

You have heard the de Grandpré Report on the Free Trade Agreement talk about the trampoline rather than the safety net. They are trying to do away with the safety net now. Give us a trampoline. Lose your job? Bounce right back! You know what happens when you bounce the wrong way on a trampoline? You break your neck and you are paralyzed from the neck down. In this case, you will be paralyzed in both directions.

In other words, in case you missed it, "sophisticated" here means, precisely, non-union, anti-union.

So where are we? We now understand half the puzzle. When corporate pronouncements call for new training and new sophisticated skills for an advanced technological economy, really what they are looking for is non-union workers, the kinds of workers who willingly adapt to ever changing new technologies without resistance, who commit themselves responsibly to company goals and who are "above" asking for anything in return. They are looking for workers who are trainable, ready and willing to be molded according to employer specifications. Such are the new skills.

## *And Now They Want Our Minds, Too*

By now, you might be asking, wait a minute aren't there some complex technical skills that employers need from their workers to run the new high tech offices and factories? Well, yes. The new information society being constructed requires not only compliant workers but also some workers with the skills to operate, monitor and troubleshoot the new technological systems.

Most of the corporate propaganda about training and new

skills refers to attitudes and values disguised as skills, as I have described them. But let's turn now to the technical skills and training of men and women on the front lines with the new technology. We will find that just as the corporate world wants our attitudes, our trust, our obedience – the hearts of union workers, it also wants our minds as well. Just as management has tried to turn workers of the industrial era into dumb, repetitive, machine-like creatures on assembly lines and office steno pools, now workers are expected to be "machines" of a different stripe, in order to interface with the new, "smart" computerized information technologies. Workers have to become a species of new smart computer technologies themselves. A sort of intelligent robot - high speed information processors. Whereas, up till now, employers tried to turn our bodies into machines to fit the pace and character of industrial machinery, now the minds of the so-called new worker are being molded to meet the high performance pace and standards of information technology surrounding them.

What am I talking about? To make clear what this is all about, I would like to go back a moment in history to the United States military in World War II where all of this started. Don't be surprised that I bring in the military here. Where, after all, do you think the new technologies in the workplace came from? All this info-age technology: computers, numerical control machining, intelligent robotics, CAD/CAM, networking, telecommunications, bioengineering, lasers. All of it originated in the military research and development over the decade since World War II and so, incidentally, have most of the educational technologies infiltrating education and training since World War II, from programmed instruction and teaching machines to computer-assisted instruction and video disc training.

You can see in the old picture on the next page the automated education envisioned by military trainers. You see the teacher there stuffing those books in the chute like a meat grinder and then it goes right into the earphones, right into the learners' heads. God, if it could only be like that. Then they would be able to control training just like they control everything else.

▲ l'École

Most of the so-called Japanese-style of manufacturing including statistical process control also comes from the work of American management consultants who developed their ideas of efficiency working for defense contractors during World War II. So the military connection is crucial here, I hope you see.

Talking about these military origins is important also for another reason because it reminds us that what is really going on now in the new corporate campaign about skills is at bottom a mobilization, a call to arms, to fight the global competitors. It's a call for solidarity – not the kind we're used to but rather a solidarity of co-operation between labour and management, to fight the common enemy to our way of life and to our standard of living. So, talk of the military here is particularly appropriate.

At the close of World War II, the head of the U.S. Air Corps Applied Psychology Panel announced that "the application of scientific method to make the material weapon fit the man and mold men to fit the weapon did more to win the war than any other activity."

"Man-machine." One word. "Man-machine is the fighting unit. Not man alone, not machine alone," he declared. Thus was born the concept of the man-machine system: the melding of man and machine. (Pardon me, I use the word man here, not woman – the military is still an extremely sexist organization in the U.S., so bear with me.)

The melding of man and machine, (I don't think women want

this anyway – do you? Neither do men.) The melding of man and machine into a single smoothly running unit. The result of new forms of engineering called human factors engineering or, more ominously, psychotechnology, psychoengineering. Now, four decades later, new weapons systems like the B1 bomber, the F15 fighter, the M1 tank, are all viewed in the military as highly complex hybrids of advanced hardware and human components.

The human is one component in a vast, highly complex technological system. Just as we used to refer to armed soldiers, now they talk about manned weapons. The human is a component.

In 1949 just after the Soviets got the bomb – a scary time – the U.S. Air Force began to develop a massive computerized air defence system for North America using some of the first computers ever built.

As they started to set up the system, they began to do practice runs with part of it. They began to realize that the key ingredient in the system, the one on which it stood or fell, was the human radar operator. The air-controller sitting in front of the radar monitor looking for those particular blips out of thousands and thousands that were coming across the screen that meant Russian planes. The testers realized that all the sophisticated technology that would eventually process this flood of incoming information for 23 centres across the continent was useless unless they could count on the human operators' correct life or death decisions about what they saw on the screen. Planners realized that they had to study the way the human mind processed information and made such decisions, and they started to look at the human operator as himself an information processing system in his own right. A sort of human computer technology inserted within a vast technological system.

Now, this model of the attentive vigilant human operator viewed as a mental, or what they called "cognitive," component in a huge computerized system is the model of the new sort of worker that corporate employers are now seeking for their high tech offices and factories. It is also the model for intelligent expert systems – the capturing of human intelligence in the machine (I will talk about that a little later).

We are now ready to look at how the corporate call for new

sophisticated skills in the high tech workplace really represents an assault, a harnessing, a kidnapping, a bending of the minds of workers, turning them into mental technologies integrated into large technological systems.

Corporate leaders tell us now that they suddenly need people who can think, who can "problem solve," who have "higher order" intellectual abilities. No longer are we told that factories and offices need mindless robots. They need mindful and creative people. Sounds great. But what do they mean? What they mean is not what they say. A leading scientist in the military computer history I have been describing, and he was also a major proponent in the computer literacy campaign, said about ten years ago, "We are retooling our industry and now we must retool ourselves." Of course he was not talking about himself. He was talking about the rest of us.

This retooling is a mental retooling, turning workers into monitors of huge computerized systems that are modelled after the continuous flow- type production now found in petrochemical, paper and utilities plants. The goal of management is to turn all manufacturing work and all office work into huge systems of continuously flowing information monitored by hand-picked mindful, attentive operators. No wonder then that one corporate consultant states "the ability to keep alert and attentive is the key job characteristic of the new age." No wonder he also says that video games are the perfect training method.

Another consultant talks about what she calls the new "intellective skills," needed by workers in the age of the smart machine: the ability to monitor continuous flows of information, to be patient because 99.9% of the time nothing significant ever happens on the screen. And vigilant, so that if anything ever goes wrong, it will be spotted. Do you want to know what this kind of work is like? I was talking to a friend of mine who does this sort of work at Xerox. He was telling me that he kind of liked the work, it really gave him control and he was able to do a lot of things at his work station that he wasn't able to do before, without moving around. But then he remembered that that very morning he had gotten really excited as two o'clock came around. Why was he excited? He had a dental appointment. He told me he hates to go to the dentist. So he said, hey, maybe I don't like doing this job after all.

Such is the new thinking, the new problem solving, the higher order intellectual skills, the ability to become an information processor inserted into the bowels of information systems. The U.S. Department of Labor report I mentioned earlier states that "the employer's competitive edge is increasingly reliant upon how effectively and efficiently information workers and information machines are integrated and moved through the production cycle together."

In short, they want us to be sort of low-level astronauts (who still ride the bus to work) – people who give their full minds to technology.

I must point out in passing that this giving one's mind to the technology is meant quite literally in another sense. I mentioned earlier that psychologists and computer scientists have been working hard trying to simulate human intelligence, trying to capture it in so-called intelligent machineries "artificial intelligence." This effort is in full swing as exemplified in the following General Motors advertisement.

It shows a picture of a mechanic staring at a computer screen over the open hood of a car, with the headline, "Now one of your mechanic's tools is another man's mind." The ad goes on to say:

> At GM, we think of computers in human terms. Because today, we have begun to program human knowledge - and logic – into a computer. It's called artificial intelligence. So, even when an engine expert retires from GM, his mind can still work for you. His lifetime of experience can go into the computer. The computer can then dispense this invaluable knowledge not only to GM engineers, but to your mechanic, too. That way, he'll be able to use this computer to help him service your car. With artificial intelligence, a lifetime of experience can now last a hundred lifetimes. Because at GM, our quest for knowledge never tires. Or retires. The GM odyssey: science not fiction.

So-called "knowledge engineers" are working day and night for their corporate bosses trying to figure out how we tick, how we make decisions, how we think, how we troubleshoot, how we know when a piece of metal can be machined and when it can't, how we somehow mysteriously know what's wrong with a piece of subtle high-performance machinery, how we perceive visual information, how we monitor a screen.

The knowledge engineers want ultimately to suck all our expertise out of us and put it all into so-called expert systems. Then they can eliminate human beings from the process altogether. So all this attention to our minds, and this need for our mental processes, all this call for education and training of workers that we are hearing now is, in management's agenda, a temporary moment. Eventually, they hope, they won't need us at all.

So now we have discovered yet another piece of the puzzle of why management emphasizes the need for sophisticated skills. Here sophisticated means mindfulness, intelligence, higher order skills, as opposed to manual, low-order repetitive intellectual functions. But it really means the molding of people's minds into information processing systems within complex computerized systems.

## *Learning: The New Labour*

There is one final, very important sense of sophisticated skill we have not yet discussed and this brings us closest to the heart of training and education. In every corporate statement about the new high tech skills, a key ingredient is flexibility, adaptability, the ability to learn continuously. This is why employers tell the schools to teach kids how to learn and they will do the rest. Sounds great. Just what we want for our kids and for our fellow workers, a lifetime of learning. Is that not what we are all here today for? To learn as much as we can? Once again however, high tech means something very different from what we are talking about.

The new high tech workplace will not only be a continuous process operation, it will also be infinitely flexible, in theory, thanks to new sophisticated technologies. Flexible manufacturing systems will some day, management hopes, permit the production of a customized, diversified product without small batch production or major retooling. The same production line will produce each car, for example, as a custom car: different colours, different models, different options on the same line, one right after another.

And with "just in time" inventories, just the right amount and kind of parts will be called up as needed for new car orders. This is the goal. You in the autoworkers union might be able to tell me how far they have gotten with this goal. Ideally, the same technology that is used to produce cars will be able to be retooled efficiently to produce a new product – truck, tank, in response to the company's product diversification initiatives.

What makes all this possible is that computerized technologies are adaptable, flexible, and, management hopes, will someday be able to retool themselves according to new product specifications. In other words, they will be able to learn. The machines, management hopes, will be able to learn.

Now, workers learning on the job amounts to the same thing. With the short life cycle of new products and the fast-paced competitive economy, workers will also have to retool themselves constantly.

Just as workers think they have learned one system or one product, they will have to start learning another. Another friend at Xerox tells me how frustrating and taxing it is for him, as part of management, that they constantly change product designs of new copiers just as he has begun to make sense of the old ones. And this changing is endless.

Not only does the short life cycle of accelerated product innovation force workers to learn continuously on line, decentralized production methods and leaner work forces call for the remaining workers to do many different jobs. Workers have to be "multi-skilled," just like the new "cashier-bagboy." Workers will have to be multi-skilled, management tells us, adaptable to any job they are assigned to.

How much technical expertise will such multi-skilled workers need to have on all these jobs? According to the same U.S. Department of Labor report on workplace skills, "although the job of the new technician responsible for all the functions performed by displaced workers may not require the same depth of skill as each of the more jobs it absorbs, it does require a wider variety of skills than any one of the other jobs."

What does this amount to? Jack-of-all-trades, master of none. Quantity substitutes for quality. The ability to learn, in other words, is a shallow substitute for real learning, the learning that leads to mastery, expertise, craftsmanship, dignity.

One corporate spokesman from the prestigious Harvard Business School tells us that in the age of the smart machine, the new labour is learning. The ability to learn and relearn new deskilled tasks is the final sophisticated skill of the new high tech workers.

As we have seen, it is a peculiar kind of learning though. As one knowledge engineer put it at a conference I recently attended, this new kind of ongoing learning is "just-in-time" learning. Continuous, on-line, fine-tuning of the human component in the computerized workplace.

In the words of yet another corporate analyst, "the delivery of relevant accessible instructional guidance will be presented by miniaturized computer-based systems that offer needed information at the precise time it is required for effective action." These "pinpointed" skills are the goal of the new learning and new training.

Note that training here has become part of the scenario of the production process. Training is a sub-system of a larger system. As someone once put it, "as we advance towards computer society, the educational and training process is likely to take on the character of real time control systems themselves." So as learning is the new labour, training is part of the new production process - the sub-system – what in the military they call the "personnel subsystem."

Perhaps the most horrible part of this is that such learning produces nothing of value for the worker. The worker does not own these many skills. He or she cannot go out and use them elsewhere. They do not give dignity or self-worth. They belong to the production process, not to the worker apart from this process. Learning and labour have become one and the same, and the worker is left with nothing but the shirt on his or her back.

## *Conclusion*

So here we have it, the unravelling of the puzzle. The new high tech corporate agenda. Now some of you might be thinking, "Hey, it's all folly, they are not going to be able to pull this thing off. I know where I work, it's all just hot air. Their vision of an automated, depopulated production process won't ever get off the ground."

Well, that's what critics are saying about the new B2 bomber, the stealth bomber, that you might have heard about in the U.S., sort of a flying wing that's inherently unstable, never been able to fly, nothing like it has been ever able to fly. Its designers have just convinced the Air Force to build, to go into full production of the stealth bomber, 23 of them at a cost of a half a billion dollars each. (You know what that could do for education?)

The two prototypes of the stealth bomber have never been flown. They can't be flown. They're not fully equipped. So they've never gotten off the ground, never been tested in flight. Why? Because the designers all believe that their sophisticated design technology that put this stealth together is capable of fully testing and simulating all the possible things that could happen to the stealth bomber in flight. Hey, you don't have to try it out! Start building them.

Here, belief is reality. If you have the power and the bucks then, whether or not your vision is a folly, you can change the world and destroy many people's lives in the process. It does not matter if it will ever get off the ground. It will destroy our lives just trying to prove that it can.

Corporate talk of sophisticated skills, then, is couched in all the right language. The same language we in the labour movement use when we talk about such things: self-esteem, motivation, a willingness to learn, thinking, problem-solving, autonomy, responsibility, flexibility, lifetime learning, mindfulness, attentiveness. As we've seen, though, the new sophisticated skills of the high tech workplace are really instruments of bewilderment, destabilization, confusion. They are "skills" in subservience and compliance and empty-headed mindfulness and meaningless, alienated learning – they are in short, the key ingredients in a new corporate assault on the hearts and minds of workers.

To conclude, I hope that whenever you hear the private sector promoting the training of workers and the education of your children, using all the right words, you will keep in mind that it is just their latest seductive, slippery, sleazy effort to beat us into submission and wipe us out.

Now we know what they are up to, and, if we in the trade union movement could start clearly to articulate what we mean by all those wonderful words, then we will know what training and education and skills mean for us. Then, we might be able to use this occasion of what management is doing as an opportunity: we will be able to use their own game against them. Then we will be ready for them.

*Doug Noble teaches in Rochester, New York, and writes extensively on the corporate/military agenda in North American schools.*

## Chapter 8

## Training For Workers, Not For Bosses

*Nancy Jackson*

Our task for this afternoon is to consider the problem of taking action – action to define and defend our own interests in the issue of training. This is a large order, but one we cannot afford to ignore. Doug Noble's presentation this morning shows us quite graphically the magnitude of problem we are facing. The insidiousness – and pervasiveness – of the dominant military/industrial logic which he describes is a sign of the urgency for a coherent response from the labour movement.

There is lots of room for debate about the specific impact of technological change on work. All the available research shows that the character of specific innovations is extremely various and contradictory from one workplace to the next. This makes it very hard to generalize. Perhaps more important, the political implications are often at least as contradictory as the technical ones. This makes it impossible to think about the relation between technological change and training needs in purely technical terms. So the first thing I have to say about a plan of action must be this: pay careful attention to the particular dynamics that are developing in your workplaces. In the end, it is those conditions that you will have to deal with and respond to in ways that meet the needs of your members.

Following this morning's presentation, I wandered around between discussion groups, listening to the stories people were telling. Many people concurred that much of the training going on in their workplaces was contradictory and divisive, disrupting relations among workers and undermining solidarity within the union. Lurking around in peoples' stories was a sense of anger and frustration. The picture is not an encouraging one. But it is the place we must start. These scattered experiences of anger and frustration are precisely the materials that we need to draw on in building a vision of alternatives in training. I will return to this point in a few minutes.

## *The Corporate Need To Train*

First, I want to make a number of observations about our collective experiences with training. If I am representing your experiences fairly, many of the things I have to say will be familiar. Some of them are so obvious that we overlook their significance altogether, but at our peril. For instance, I think we ought to give more political significance to the fact that companies are more and more anxious to train. They want to do 'corporate culture' training; they want to do 'management' training; they want to do 'personal effectiveness' training such as stress management or time management; and they want to do training for technical 'skills upgrading'. Not only do corporations want to do all this training, but governments want to help them do it. This sense of urgency, the imperative to train, is a brief historical moment with enormous political potential. We need to put it to work for us.

It can work for us because it can't be accomplished without us. That is, the employers' desire to train is not just an abstract idea. They need to train US in particular, and they can't do that without some level of participation and agreement on our part. At the moment they are quite successfully securing that participation in a very piecemeal fashion, even on an individual basis. Most of what I want to talk about is setting some terms for participation that are more collective and reflect our own agenda on the issue of training.

Employers want to train us because the global economic climate in which they conduct their business is changing. So they are reorganizing their management styles–talking about quality circles and team concepts. They are changing their production methods–introducing "just-in-time" delivery systems and "continuous flow" production, and so on. They are changing the kinds of technology being used in order to remain competitive: computer-assisted design; computer-numeric controls; electronic data transfer and communication systems ... the list goes on and on. What matters most to us it that all of these changes in the way the employer is doing business lead to changes in how they want us to work. They want us to know how to operate their computerized machines, and to do so with ever greater speed and precision, leading to ever greater productivity, etc. We see and hear these requirements being articulated all the time in policy documents and media reports.

## *A Worker-Management Struggle*

So, the second major point I want to make is this. When we talk about training "needs", let's be a little careful about whose "needs" we are talking about: ours or the employers? Training "needs" are not absolute or universal. They are not dictated from heaven or by some natural force of history. They arise as the product of certain kinds of managerial and technological choices that employers are making. So we should think of them, not as "needs" in some absolute sense, but as the employers' 'shopping list'–as the set of demands employers are making for training. Both their choices and the training demands to which they lead should be the object of our constant critical appraisal.

In the long run, we need alternatives to the choices employers are making about managerial and technical organization in the workplace. But at the moment, the arena of struggle that is available to us is around training. The alternative to simply accepting employers' training demands is to ask ourselves, what are the "needs" of workers in the face of the changes management is adopting? What are our needs related to the new technical and managerial methods? What are our own "needs" when it comes to training? How could training be used to strengthen our position? In each of our workplaces, we need to begin to think through exactly these questions. Only when we have done so will we be in a position to talk with the employer community about training. Only then will we be in a position to formulate some terms and conditions for our participation in the kinds of training they want.

In other words, the first step is to get back into a bargaining frame of mind! Let's stop assuming that somebody else has the right to dictate training "needs". Let's start defining an approach to training which is truly on our side instead of absolutely and unequivocally on their side.

## *A Void In Our Knowledge*

The next problem we face is the huge void of knowledge about training initiatives that represent the interests of workers. Certainly in North America, this void is really shocking. I have spent the last five years searching libraries and talking to educators in various places in the country, and I am convinced that our collective expertise in this area is weak at best. In other parts of the world, this is not so true. In Germany and the Scandinavian countries, for example, there is a relatively long and honourable history of expertise about worker-centred approaches to vocational and technical learning both on and off the job. But we have not imported these approaches or that expertise to North America. Instead, we are presently in the business of borrowing heavily from Japan, where there is also an enormous wealth of experience and expertise about training. But it is almost exclusively management oriented. That is, it reflects managements' interests in the labour process, and approaches the training of labour exclusively in that light. This is the model which is gaining currency in the training field in North America.

So, in many ways, we are forging new territory for Canadian labour relations. We are asking questions that we haven't asked before, and we need answers that we haven't heard before. For example, as you well know, Canada has in the past relied heavily on immigration for its supply of skilled labour. As a result, there are many areas of technical expertise, essential to the functioning of the Canadian economy, for which we haven't developed a very elaborate training apparatus either in industry or in our public educational institutions. It is only in the past ten years that we have begun to see a growing public interest in developing training programs in many of these areas.

## Corporate Dominance

But there is a still a problem. The problem is that the schemes being introduced to address these training needs are not good news for working people. They heavily favour the private sector employer, not only as the site of training but also as the source of expertise on learning needs and as the mechanism for design and delivery of training. Just as one piece of evidence of this trend, I refer you to a report recently published by the federal government, which is a study of 120 private training corporations that have been in existence for five to ten years. The study looks at who these training companies are serving and what they are offering, and it reports not surprisingly, that the biggest client group is management, and that approximately 70% of their courses are management training courses. Just the very existence of 120 private training corporations is itself an indication of the kind of 'learning for profit' framework within which training expertise is being generated. This arrangement is unlikely to represent our interests as workers very well.

Similar problems exist with the mechanisms being set up within government itself. They are oriented to serving business, by which they do not mean you and me. The policy literature over recent months proposes and puts in place layer after layer of administrative mechanisms oriented to servicing employers' needs, many of which are training-related. The example which always sticks in my mind is the creation of the not-so-old federal Department of Industry, Science and Technology. If you read their mandate, it's wording is very clear. Their job is to develop a "systematic intelligence-gathering and review process related to advocacy and policy for business". My point is that millions of dollars, including public dollars, are being spent developing an expertise about 'the needs of industry' in the present economic climate, but it's all on the other side.

## Management Centred Training

So, let's take a closer look at the products of this kind of development process in the area of training, a development process in which the voice of labour is largely silenced. To do this, I will draw on bits and pieces of information from the discussion groups this morning. And I will draw on material from some interesting and innovative research being done at the present time in the Ontario labour movement. In particular I want to acknowledge the work of the Canadian Auto Workers researchers Dave Robertson and Jeff Wareham. Their work is particularly important because it gives a great deal of visibility into the changing dynamics of the labour process in a wide range of workplaces here in Ontario, where both technological and managerial changes are well advanced. Their careful analysis lets us see the implications of those changes for workers.

I am also going to focus on problems related to technical skills training in particular because this is still the hardest nut to crack. Much more critical work has already been done on training oriented to developing "corporate culture". This would include various critiques of Quality of Working Life programs, such as Don Wells' book *Empty Promises*, which you should read if you haven't already, or critiques of the team concept such as the handbook for unionists *Choosing Sides* written by American researchers Mike Parker and Jane Slaughter. There are also good courses available in the labour movement that directly address these issues. I am thinking in particular of courses designed by unionists like Bruce May, D'Arcy Martin and Rick Williams, which deal with the problems encountered in facing these management initiatives in our workplaces. But when it comes to technical skills training, we easily fall back into some old ways of thinking. We fall back into the assumption that technology itself is determining training "needs", that it is all part and parcel of scientific progress, and that all we can do is follow along and learn how to run these newfangled machines in order to save our jobs. If our thinking starts there, we have already lost the battle.

## *Controlling Our Work Through Health and Safety*

Let me start with an example of management centred training which may have elements familiar to many of you. The example is actually from the area of health and safety, but it has a peculiar and important hybrid character to which I want to draw your attention. I refer you to a *Globe and Mail* article from April 29, 1989 which talks about safety training for forestry workers in Ontario. I don't know the background to this particular case, but I see in the Globe that loggers are now going to be required to participate in a new form of safety training in order to reduce accidents in their industry, which, we are reminded, has the highest rate of deaths and disabling accidents in the province. These are matters of gravest concern to all of us.

But what catches my attention in this story is that the courses are going to be compulsory in order for workers to be considered "certified" for their job, and that industry spokespersons expect the training to "improve workers' productivity at the same time". Improved productivity is a reasonable expectation insofar as accidents usually mean down-time for the employer as well as personal injury for the worker. What concerns me about this initiative is the rather complex and contradictory way in which our interests in better protection in the area of health and safety are being piggy-backed onto the employers' interests in redefining how we do our work. So health and safety training becomes an occasion for the employer to have another crack at reshaping the standards for and methods of control over our work, and for making this kind of retraining a condition for holding our jobs. Such initiatives may not be purely good news for forestry workers.

## *Whose Time Is Used?*

A second common problem is the issue of whose time is used for training. The newspaper article on health and safety training for forestry workers does not tell us whether the new compulsory training will be conducted on the employers' time or the employees' own time. But how often have I read in the last few years about compulsory training which is done exclusively on the employees' off hours, with or without subsidy to cover direct costs. In some cases, such after-hours training only secures the workers the privilege of bidding for the newly reorganized form of their old jobs. This is a practice which deserves to be nipped in the bud. It essentially means that the responsibility for the disruptive effects of new management strategies and new production methods are being shifted to workers by redefining the problem as their lack of qualifications. You are qualified for your job today, but tomorrow you are not qualified. It is the job that has changed, but it's treated as your problem. This kind of political sleight of hand is so commonplace that we don't even get excited about it. We see it as a perfectly legitimate, rather than a highly uncivilized, way to manage a labour market.

## Apprenticeship and Mastery

Of course, struggles over time are also closely related to questions about the type and content of training that should be available to Canadian workers. These battles take many forms, but one of the clearest examples is the issue of apprenticeships. Over the last decade, we have watched the steady erosion of comprehensive forms of apprenticeship training, and their replacement by various so-called "flexible" forms of certification which allow the worker to be deployed in a much more management-friendly fashion on the shop floor. Even though the Ontario government has been making a lot of promises in the past year or so about rebuilding and revitalizing the apprenticeship system, we can see simply by looking that they have not really been delivering on this promise. If and when they do, we can be certain that the form of apprenticeships they have in mind will not include the very strong structure of protections for the worker which have been built into the licensing of trades people in the past, and will not provide the same bargaining power on the shop floor.

But the decline of the old concept of apprenticeships poses more problems that immediately meet the eye. That is, it marks the loss of the whole concept of 'mastery' as something that belongs to the worker, individually or collectively. Instead, we find ourselves increasingly on a terrain where questions about the nature of work, how it should be organized, what is safe and what isn't etc. are wholly the prerogative of management. Answers to these important questions are moved ever more deeply into management territory. Once lost, this ground will be very difficult to regain.

Of course, battles over training content are far more widespread than the case of apprenticeships. The general trend seems to be that employers are primarily interested in doing "applications" types of training – programs that deal with specific operations and procedures for particular equipment used under routine conditions. And even in this kind of training, companies are given to a form of cost cutting that we might call "quick and dirty" training. The most common version of this syndrome is the reliance on vendor training. That is, the employer buys a new piece of equipment for a purchase price that includes a certain number of hours of training for a certain number of employees. The employer is convinced by the vendor that "even a monkey" will be able to run that equipment based on these few hours of training, etc. Aside from the outrageous slight to workers of this common kind of talk, it masks a number of problems in the workplace. Dave Robertson and Jeff Wareham describe this problem very nicely when they say something like, "...it is true that very sophisticated equipment can sometimes, and for a while, and under certain circumstances be run by people with very limited training". But that is not the end of the story. Over the long haul and in non-routine circumstances, this kind of impoverishment in the understanding of shop floor workers will not give us safe, efficient or productive workplaces, and it will not give us interesting and fulfilling work.

## *Workers Want To Know Why*

Meanwhile, there is ample research which shows that workers in all types of workplaces have a desire to learn not only what they have to do, but also why. They want to know not just the rote mechanics but also the underlying sense of the work processes of which they are a part, so they can act safely, responsibly and intelligently on the job. It is here, however, that employers are most resistant. On the whole the employer community shows little willingness to undertake the kinds of training that could be called employee development, or learning which could be seen as a long-term investment in the smooth operation of the production process. This kind of learning they expect to take place at the tax payers' expense or at the expense of individual job seekers.

The question of who will pay for training is in part a thinly disguised problem of cost accounting. That is, training expenses are currently counted as a cost item for business. But accounting practices are not written in stone, as we are reminded with every new budget. If there were a public will to do so, training costs could be treated as an investment in the health of our economy, and be made eligible for the same kind of tax breaks and financial incentives that are currently applied to other expenses of doing business, such as investment in new capital equipment. Until that happens, comprehensive and developmental training will continue to be at the bottom of the employers' priority list.

Finally, there are many trouble spots around the question of access to training. Since skills upgrading is ever more closely tied to chances for continuing employment and promotion, questions of access are consequential for workers in both the long and the short run. Here again, access is commonly controlled by management, and organized to serve their interests. There is often preferential access to training for excluded workers as opposed to bargaining unit members, or preferential access of younger workers with better educational backgrounds, or male workers rather than female workers etc. Management control of decision-making means those workers who best serve management's purposes are the ones who get the training. Until we gain more control over access to training, this situation can be expected to continue.

## *Claiming Our Knowledge*

Another form of selective training is the popular scheme under which management picks out a handful of workers to receive formal instruction, and then sends them back to "pass their skills along to their fellow workers." When you hear that kind of talk in your workplace, you know you are in trouble.

Because "passing the skills along" means both delivering training and receiving training without getting credit for either. Participating in these arrangements both obscures and undermines the knowledge-base in the office or on the shop floor. What we need to do instead is to claim and protect that knowledge as the basis of our power, rather than to give it away through management-driven forms of "cooperation".

Overall, then, many of our training troubles seem to stem from the fact that unions currently have very little purchase on training decisions. In this morning's discussion groups I heard people say over and over, "We haven't managed to get much in the way of general training provisions negotiated into our contract." Indeed from workplace to workplace, the same thing is true, and I think we need to take more seriously the scope and significance of this problem.

We haven't easily won a voice in training decisions because this territory is a critical frontier in the employers' plans for work reorganization. In redesigning the work process, they are redesigning jobs, and they need training programs to supply them with the appropriate forms of skilled labour. So control over training is very central to their agenda. Meanwhile, as they redesign work and jobs, they are also eliminating the basis for the structure of protections which we have won over the last 50 years—the credentials and job classifications that have been the foundation of our collective agreements. When they train us out of these forms of work, they train us out of these important sources of power in the workplace. The stakes are very high, and training is the vehicle.

So, the important thing to remember is that training is not just about knowledge or skill; it is about power. If we separate the two, we are walking like a lamb to the slaughter. I think Doug Noble said it very well this morning in the last few moments of his presentation. He said something like "The biggest problem we face is that learning and labour are coming to be one and the same thing. And as they become the same, they both belong to production. When that happens, there is nothing left for the worker." I agree absolutely with this formulation of the problem. Learning is coming to be treated as part of the labour process, and as such is coming more and more under management control. And when our knowing, our very capacity to know, becomes as much the property of capital as the product of our labour, what do we have left? Where do we have to stand? We can't afford to underestimate the significance of this struggle.

## A Worker-Centred Alternative

This litany of troubles looks pretty bleak. So let's turn our attention to thinking about alternatives. What would a more worker-centred approach to training look like? Again, I want to pass on to you some of the thinking about this question that is currently being done within the Ontario labour movement. This thinking reflects experience in the aerospace industry, the auto industry, and electronics industry and elsewhere. In particular, I am again drawing most heavily on the work of CAW researchers Dave Robertson and Jeff Wareham, because their thinking on these questions is the most advanced I have seen.

The central theme for a worker-centred approach to training seems to be that training needs to be open to everyone. No more preferential access controlled by management. No more quotas that privilege the youngest or the fittest or the whitest or the most management-friendly corners of the workforce. Training or retraining needs to be a basic right, a part of working life that is as routine as the work we do. Different kinds of training need to be available to workers with different needs, and workers do the choosing. At the same time, training needs to be explicit: countable and counted, recognized, paid, credited. No more of this business of "go back and show your buddies".

Secondly, the details of a training plan ought to be co-determined between labour and management, including the contents, the delivery methods, the timing, etc. We should hold out for training based on more democratic principles of adult education, drawing on models used in other jurisdictions where we lack expertise of our own.

Thirdly, training should be developmental for the worker. That is, we shouldn't settle for training that teaches us only how to operate a particular piece of equipment within a tight set of performance parameters. Instead, training should expand our knowledge of the work process, so that it helps us not only do the job we have, but also get the next promotion. We need to demand forms of skill training that increase our mobility in the labour market, rather than tying us down to a particular job or even a particular employer. This is of course a very contentious demand, and one that leads to my next major point.

That is, we need to protect the principle of public education. This means access to training in the public realm and access to credentials that have a currency on a free labour market. I heard a number of stories in workshops this morning about workplace-specific licensing practices. I feel enormously nervous about this practice, particularly in light of the encroachment of Japanese-style labour relations in which both training and credentials are company-specific, leading to a virtually captive labour force. In Japan, individuals do not work for one employer from cradle to grave simply out of an overly-developed sense of loyalty. They do so in part because their credentials are not recognized by other employers. To the extent that we move in the direction of making the learning and the credentialing process the property of the employer, we are altering very fundamentally the contract between labour and capital which we have enjoyed on this continent. That is something we need to think very carefully about.

Finally, I want to place an item on the agenda that I will call "knowledge engineering", to borrow another term from Doug Noble. The kind of "knowledge engineering" I have in mind is part of up-dating the labour relations framework within which we work. That is, we need to find the time and resources to devise an entirely fresh approach to a "structure of protections" around our jobs, one that is not a hold-over from working conditions of the past, but adequately reflects and represents our interests in the newly reorganized workplaces of the present. Such a new approach to a structure of protections needs to be firmly attached to any agreements we make about training for new forms of work. Only under these conditions will we emerge from the retraining process stronger than we went in.

## *Building Our Strength*

Now, the biggest problem we still face is this. If management were to come to us tomorrow and say, "OK, let's co-determine. What do you want in training?" we wouldn't have a ready answer. We do not have the expertise, ready and waiting, to know what to demand. We have yet to put flesh on the skeleton agenda I have been talking about today. Such demands must be formulated on an industry by industry basis, workplace by workplace, based on an intimate understanding of the dynamics of change in each place. So, in the few minutes that remain, I want to turn my attention to the problem of building an infrastructure of local knowledge as the foundation for a worker-centred approach to training.

Here I am particularly indebted to the work of Marie Campbell, an Ottawa-based researcher and educator who has for a number of years been doing very interesting and innovative work with nurses unions across the country, as well as some other public sector workers. Judging from the exceptional results that nurses are having in educating and mobilizing their members, this way of working must have something to recommend it.

We have to begin by turning the tables on some common wisdom. That is, we have for a long time subscribed to a pervasive cultural myth that answers always come from the experts. We believe that somebody will come along and know how to design the machines that work better, or will organize work more humanely. We want experts to tell us how to design personnel systems or labour relations frameworks that are accountable to workers needs. We look to experts for better designs for health and safety in our workplace. We hope against hope that these answers will just walk in the door one day, and all we will have to do is pay for them. But if we look a little more closely at our own experience, we can see the fallacy of this way of thinking. We know perfectly well that the experts have let us down pretty badly in the past. We have all worked with machines that were badly designed. We have all been in work places where the work flow was poorly organized, where time and materials were wasted. We have all suffered under decisions that were slow and arbitrary, and often didn't address the problems they were meant to solve. Even the complex labour relations framework to which we cling for lack of an alternative hasn't been perfect. It has permitted workers to be divided against one another, women and non-white workers to be routinely undervalued, scores of workers to be injured and discarded, and so forth.

## *Relying On Our Own Knowledge*

The alternative to depending on expert answers is to rely on ourselves. To recognize that the best source of expertise for building worker-friendly environments is workers. Whether we want to design more interesting jobs, more adequate and rewarding training programs, safer work places, or stronger mechanisms for worker input into decision-making, the place to start is with our own good common sense and collective experience. We need to assemble what we already know, the knowledge and understanding you and I acquire every day as we go about our jobs, between breakfast and lunch, between lunch and coffee break, between cigarettes. We need to begin to see the strategic value of that knowledge.

Now, the problem is, of course, that employers have already noticed that the real expertise about the work process is on the shop floor. That is why they have you sitting around in little circles telling them what you know. So what I want to say is simple: why are we sitting around in little circles talking to management when we could be sitting around in little circles talking to our unions? It is the union that most needs to hear the kind of knowledge you have about the machines you operate, the safety issues related to your work station, the training needs you can identify, the job mobility you seek, etc. The union needs this information because they are the only people whose job it is to work for you instead of against you. It's that simple.

So I want to argue that we should indeed be sitting around in little circles–whether it happens on or off the job. We should be harnessing the shop floor knowledge of all your members, collectivizing and systematizing what you already know, and giving it back to management over the bargaining table, not in quality circles.

We know lots of things that could form the basis for bargaining positions around training. We can see the strengths and weakness of the work organization in our places of employment. We can see what kinds of training would improve our jobs and strengthen the relations between workers in our places of work. What changes would it take, for example, in training practices in your workplace so that whole groups of your fellow workers were not being dead-ended in their jobs? What kind of training would it take to let clerical workers in your offices stop using microcomputers like glorified typewriters? We see these things happening all around us, and we see that they are unnecessary and costly in both financial and human terms. But we have no place, no vehicle to use our knowledge.

There is nothing new in proposing that we sit around in little circles talking to each other as unionists. There are a number of initiatives in the Ontario labour movement right now that work in this way: we call them 'education delegates' or 'technology reps' or 'local discussion leaders'–the variations are potentially endless. Such schemes have enormous potential to improve communication at the level of the rank and file. And they have the potential to provide a little path of intelligence through which our collective wisdom can be translated into collective action. Because however brilliant our leaders are, they can't do it all for us. In the end the power of the union depends upon the members.

Taking back our shop floor knowledge in order to confront management in a negotiating process instead of giving it away in quality circles is not a very revolutionary idea. But it is pretty ambitious. It will require some work, some planning, and some cooperation. And it will require some political horse sense. We can't take on such a venture on a piecemeal basis. We can't go after one employer at a time, trying to take back some ground on the training issue. We have to move together, as a block. We have a labour central; we need to use it. We need to make the employer community a training offer they can't refuse. It's a long shot, but what's the alternative?

In closing, I would like to quote Daniel Benedict, who has a lot more experience at this game than I have. He asks, "If the trade unions won't take up the fight for a more democratic approach to education and training for workers, who will?"

*Nancy Jackson currently teaches in the Faculty of Education at McGill University and has written widely on the issue of skills training.*

# Chapter 9

# Taking Charge Of Our Future

### Julie Davis

When Gord Wilson talked about his personal experiences in school at the opening of this conference, my stomach hurt. The memories he evoked in me were all too real and still too painful.

Doug Little came over to Jim Turk and said that Gord's story was the story of his life, too. Many of the rest of you have made clear that, while the specifics may have been different, your experiences were very much the same.

This makes me angry:

- angry about the damaged lives and about the many people who did not have this damage undone (at least, in part, as I did or as Gord did) by positive experiences in the trade union movement, or by other events in their lives.
- angry that despite obvious competence and success in later life, this horrible treatment in school continues to hurt us leaving a sore that never fully heals;
- angry that the failure of the school system got explained as our failure and explained so successfully that many of us believed it;
- angry that, as George Martell made clear, these practices continue, but in a more sophisticated, slippery manner – justified by a legion of psycho-educational consultants, social workers, psychologists, and such like – and, as John Huot noted, they occur in colleges as well as elementary and secondary schools;
- angry that this treatment was reserved primarily for working class kids whose only fault was their working class background;

• angry, most of all, because all of this is so far from what can be. As Penny Moss made clear, what can be is real equality of outcome.

We should be struck, she reminded us, by the fact that virtually every child successfully completes the most difficult learning task of their entire lives without the help of schools or professionals. She was referring to learning their first language – how to speak and to understand what is being spoken to them.

Almost all kids perform this wonderful intellectual achievement before they reach school age. They all enter school having already demonstrated an amazing capacity to learn. Yet, they leave school far more unequal than when they entered.

Penny gave us some concrete ideas about how we can change this so as to begin to assure we do achieve an equality of outcome by the time children are ready to leave school.

Doug Little showed us what a wonderful teacher can do to help students learn, and he described seven elements which are key aspects of real change — things like organizing parents; more appropriate curriculum; teaching approaches that use cooperative learning practices and better student-staff ratios.

Richard Johnston made clear that the trade union movement must take real leadership on this issue if there ever is to be change. He described this conference as the beginning of a revolution in education – a phrase that as a trade union leader and social democrat warms the cockles of my heart.

But he also cautioned us that our meeting will only be meaningful if we go back to our local unions, our schools and our communities and take the initiative on education.

That is a challenge that I and the Federation take very seriously.

The OFL will be proud to be among ten or twenty or thirty labour groups appearing before the Ontario Select Committee on Education this fall when it discusses school financing – instead of being the only labour organization to appear.

It will be a great day when local unions get involved in the NDP education policy review process. Richard mentioned that he was mailing material to every New Democrat. I will send every one of you a copy of this material and urge you to get your locals involved. It is terribly important that you help your local begin to discuss the issues we have discussed at this conference. We need more of the labour movement involved. We will help. The OFL will provide speakers, material, and advice.

And think how wonderful it will be when the trade union movement provides the impetus for real educational change – change that will only occur if we all play an active role.

I look forward to the day when our movement recognizes that many trade unionists are also parents, and when we find ways, locally and provincially, to get more working class parents active and involved in schools – exercising their rights which have been largely hidden from them.

## *Making A Commitment*

We must leave this conference with a commitment to ourselves to change our educational system so that every child gets a good, meaningful education.

As George Martell so eloquently put it:

> Secretaries and plumbers, steelworkers and retail workers, mechanics and clerks must also be historians and economists, poets and scientists, intellectuals and artists. It is only through these activities that they can be full citizens – capable of powerful and purposeful work and community action. Many workers try to carry on these tasks, but they are running deeply against the grain of what the society expects of them. We have to fight for schools which open our kids to all these activities – to give them a real education.

We must leave this conference with the realization that our own unions must be a primary vehicle for educational change. We must leave this conference with an understanding that our kind of unionism means that public education is a trade union issue – that in many ways it affects everything else we do as unionists and it affects everything we are and will be.

We must also leave this conference with a new commitment to deal just as forcefully with the issue of training.

As Doug Noble made so clear to us this morning, the corporate agenda is attempting to reduce us to human components in complex technological systems – ever vigilant, attentive information processors integrated into the technological system.

Formerly, the production process tried to turn our bodies into machines. Their new production process is based on turning our minds into information processors.

The fact they advocate these changes using our language about education and training may have blinded us to what is going on.

Their talk of "lifelong learning", "flexibility and adaptability", and "continuous learning" means other than the simple meaning of those words. I hope this conference has helped us see this, and to realize that these words mask a vision of workers as imperfect computers who must be programmed and reprogrammed to meet the needs of the technologically sophisticated production process – at least until they can develop artificial intelligence or technological alternatives.

Their agenda is, as Doug suggested, to suck the expertise out of us and put it into expert systems and then get rid of us. I would urge you to look again at that General Motors advertisement which Doug distributed.

## *What's To Be Done*

The corporate call for training is, indeed, a temporary moment.

But during that moment, we have a lot to do. Let me list three things.

The first is to expose the corporate agenda. I think Doug Noble did a brilliant job of that. I hope you see that his speech gets read by people in your organization, and that you help organize discussion around it.

We need to identify how what Doug was discussing applies in different industries so we get a much more detailed picture of what workers across Ontario are facing.

We need to help people see what all this means to them.

We need to help people see that reorganized jobs may be tough. Those of you who work on the new technologies know the peculiar combination of boredom, extreme tension, pride in the use of expensive technology and heightened pressure that makes up your work life, while at the same time undermining your future job security and diminishing your intellectual and creative technical expertise.

Doug referred to an American writer who used the term "intellective" to describe many of the new work skills – as opposed to "intellectual".

And, he referred to the corporate suggestion that video games are a wonderful training tool. Anyone who has played video games can understand the distinction between intellective and intellectual. Video games are mentally demanding, physically draining but also intellectually empty. They are not the model for the kind of work that the trade union movement would ever want anyone to have to do – high-tech, air-conditioned versions of sweatshops.

We have to defend the worker stuck in those kinds of jobs and make clear that the many skills that are necessary to survive in this highly demanding environment are not the same as technical expertise that makes a job rewarding, that gives workers power and dignity.

I recognize that these are difficult issues to talk about, but we must engage in that discussion so that the true corporate agenda can be exposed. Only then can we go on to try to change it.

## *Labour's Agenda*

Our second task is to figure out what we, as workers and trade unionists, want from training – what our agenda is. I am not talking about how training should be administered.

Let me add, however, that it is my conviction that public educational institutions must play a central role in job training if a workers' training agenda is ever to be realized.

I am talking about our goals for training.

I am talking about our vision of what work should be and how training helps achieve that vision.

I am talking about training that helps equip workers with skills that enrich and empower us and enhance our collective abilities – not training that weakens and divides us so we become more compliant and helpless tools in management's reorganized work processes.

## *Organizing An Education*

As Nancy Jackson correctly pointed out, training is not just about knowledge, it is also always about power.

That is why our third task is to mobilize as a labour movement to get what we want. We will never get what we have been talking about here unless we mobilize and struggle for it.

How do we set our goals for training, our vision of what we want and how do we develop the methods by which we attempt to get it?

Again, Nancy pointed the way.

The place where the knowledge lies is among the rank-and-file in the workplace. As labour organizations we must do much more than we have in the past to find ways to draw on that knowledge – to get our members, as Nancy so aptly put it, sitting in circles not with management but with each other and their union's leaders and staff.

Our goals, our agenda, our means to implement that agenda must come from harnessing the expertise among workers in the workplace, putting that information together systematically, and then collectively giving that back to management as a demand for training that is training we want, training that is worker-centered, training that will build expertise and the power to put that expertise to use.

I believe the OFL has a major role to play in this process.

This conference is the beginning.

If you feel this is worthwhile – and I hope you do – we want to begin to develop an action plan in conjunction with the Education Committee and the Executive Board and Council to take back education and training as our issues.

Equally, I hope each of you will make a report to your local on this conference, and get your brothers and sisters thinking about what your local can do.

I hope this will lead to discussions more broadly within your whole union about how the labour movement can move forward on education and training.

I also hope you will share the thoughts within your local and within your union with the Federation so we can all move forward together.

This conference can be the beginning of the revolution in education and training that Richard Johnston referred to yesterday. Or, it can be just another conference. The decision rests with you.

*Julie Davis was formerly a national representative of the Canadian Union of Public Employees and is currently the Secretary-Treasurer of the Ontario Federation of Labour.*

# *Appendices*

# *Where We Stand:*

**Submissions to the
Ontario Select Committee
on Education
from the
Ontario Federation of Labour**

*Appendix I*

# "WHAT OUR SOCIETY NEEDS IS A BROADENING OF CREATIVE INTELLECTUAL WORK TO ALL STUDENTS, NOT A REDUCTION OF EDUCATION TO JOB TRAINING."

SUBMISSION TO
THE ONTARIO SELECT COMMITTEE ON EDUCATION
FROM THE ONTARIO FEDERATION OF LABOUR,
JULY 21, 1988

## INTRODUCTION

The educational system in Ontario is under attack from a variety of quarters. Business complains that students are not being trained adequately for the workplace. Many parents are complaining that their children are not getting a good enough education and that too many are dropping out of school. Teachers are complaining about unrealistically large class sizes and inadequate resources.

With increasing frequency, we hear calls for a "return to the basics", for "province-wide tests", for "discipline", for a "more structured curriculum."

The creation of this select committee is another reflection that education is in a period of re-evaluation.

On behalf of the 800,000 workers represented by the Ontario Federation of Labour, we appreciate the opportunity to appear before the Committee to discuss general educational issues. We hope to be able to return in September to address more specific programmatic suggestions.

## THE CHANGING PURPOSE OF EDUCATION

While education historically was the preserve of a small elite, the advent of mass education in the Nineteenth Century saw a redefinition of the goal of education. Largely divorced from its tie to high culture and academic learning, public education was supported largely on the basis that it would prepare the masses to be dutiful citizens and dutiful employees.

The Winnipeg Board of Education clearly summarized the new view in 1913:

> Until a comparatively recent period, the schools were organized on purely academic lines and the avowed aim of education was culture and discipline. This aim has, however, been greatly enlarged within the past few years, by including within its scope the development of a sense of social and civic duty, the stimulation of national and patriotic spirit, the promotion of public health, and the direct preparations for the occupations of life.

The emphasis, as Professor Ken Osborne puts it in a forthcoming book, has been on "loyalty, obedience and conformity."

A comment by a high school student nicely illustrates the point:

> You can't put up your hand and say, 'Sir, this lesson's very boring.' You just aren't allowed to do that in school. If you feel it's boring, you think there is something wrong with you; you get worried because everybody else is writing things down. Everybody is telling you what's best for you and what ain't, but you're never taught to question anything. You're taught to think like that. If you do question anything, there's something wrong with you: you're insolent, you're naughty, you're a thug.

While the goals of education, as currently set out by the Ontario Ministry of Education, bear little resemblance to the explicit demand for conformity to dominant values and practices in society and in the workplace, the education system operates in a manner as if these Nineteenth Century goals were still in place. This historic understanding of education lies behind complaints demanding that the schools produce even more conformity to the status quo.

Canada, like the rest of the Western world, has entered an extended period of economic crisis since the early 1970's, resulting in growing pressures on the educational system.

The dramatic shifts in the work world – the decline of manufacturing; the growth of office, professional, and managerial jobs; the enormous increase of women in the work force, primarily in the low-paid sectors; the growth of unemployment, particularly for the young; intensified regional inequality; and the growing dependence of the Canadian economy on the United States – have caused significant social changes and made an impact on our schools.

In this context, there are those who want the educational system to be primarily a source of stability at the expense of a deeper commitment to a critical and substantial curriculum.

It is important that the Select Committee distance itself from the immediate social pressures that have forced the educational system into the limelight so that the Committee can deal with the fundamental question: what do we want our educational system to do? Only then can we determine which, if any, current critics are justified. Only then can we intelligently discuss what to do.

## EDUCATIONAL GOALS

We in the Ontario Federation of Labour are clear about our goals for the educational system. Those goals are not narrow. For us, the principal goals are to equip everyone with the basic ability to acquire information, to reason clearly, to think critically, to communicate one's ideas effectively, and to try to put one's ideas and knowledge into practice.

These are not inconsistent with the current "Goals of Education" as enunciated by the Ontario Ministry of Education. But they are a far cry from what is actually happening in the school system.

To understand this disparity, it is necessary to go beyond stated goals to the conceptions that lie behind the goals.

### 1. THE NEED TO ELIMINATE CLASS BIAS

While our goals are compatible with the Ministry's stated goals, both are contrary to the system's apparent real goal of fostering "loyalty, obedience and conformity".

Only in programs for the elite is one likely to find some emphasis on critical thinking and expression – though it has its limitations even in these programs.

We feel everyone needs a critical education, and we feel it is time to end the class-based discrimination that restricts "good" education to an elite.

The discrimination starts in the preschool years. Before children are allowed to enter school, working class children are often put at a disadvantage because they are denied access to high quality child care. Because of a shortage of affordable spaces in good child care centres, workers' children are often forced into arrangements where they receive custodial services with little or no educational experience.

When they enter elementary school, almost all children are quickly put into homogeneous "ability" groupings – allegedly for their own good. But extensive research in Canada and the United States makes clear that "ability" grouping sorts more by social class than by any measure of intellectual ability or aptitude. And there is no clear indication that "ability" grouping achieves any worthwhile educational goal.

The "ability" grouping of elementary school turns into formal program streams in secondary school – with working class children forming almost the entirety of the two bottom streams. And what children learn in the advanced stream is quite different from what they learn in the general or basic streams.

The inequality culminates in post-secondary education where the children of high status parents constitute the overwhelming majority of university students and a disproportionate percentage of college students. Unless one holds the untenable view that working class children are less bright than their more affluent counterparts, this pattern of inequality shows something is desperately wrong with our educational system.

## 2. THE NEED TO AVOID REDUCING EDUCATION TO TRAINING

Also concomitant with our goals is a rejection of the notion that education should be narrowed to training for a job. As the economic crisis continues into its second decade, employers and governments are increasingly putting pressure on the educational system to become more explicitly a producer of willing and able workers.

We are repeatedly told that our "ability to compete", even our "economic future", depends on building a closer link between business and the education system; making sure that students have the skills and attitudes to fit the employers' current needs for workers.

While we want our children to be able to get jobs, we feel it is a large jump to the position that training is synonymous with education. In our view, there is already too close a link between business and the schools. Employers' views of the world infuse too much of the curriculum from kindergarten to university.

The irony is that in the current era of rapid social change one's ability to think creatively and critically will be more important than ever – a point that corporate human resource managers love to make when they speak on education. What they fail to say is that they want these skills as long as they are applied only to what the employer sanctions. Just as in school, so in the workplace for all but those at the top, loyalty, obedience, and conformity are what is demanded. The trade union leadership is full of bright, creative, critical thinkers who had trouble in school and in the workplace precisely because they did not restrict their critical and creative skills to what school officials and employers deemed appropriate.

Closer ties to business will inject even more restriction on genuine intellectual endeavour. What our society needs is a broadening of creative intellectual work to all students, not a reduction of education to job training.

Hopefully, we can build a society in which economic advancement will be related to a more broadly and critically educated population, not to a more narrowly trained workforce.

## 3. THE NEED TO LINK THEORY AND PRACTICE

The issue of the linkage of theory and practice is vital to all we have discussed so far. The prevailing educational approach is to separate theory and practice.

OSIS [the provincial guidelines for Intermediate and Secondary Schools] explicitly reserves theory to those in the advanced stream. An emphasis on practice is prescribed for the rest.

We reject the distinction. There is no knowledge without theory. And there is no knowledge without practice. Pretending the two can be separated is not only bad educational philosophy, it also serves as an underpinning for an two-tier educational system—theory for the best and practice for the rest.

The dichotomy also serves to mask the ideology that lies behind the supposedly pure "practice". When working class kids in the lower streams are told the values of a practical education – and often put into work situations – the ideology which guides the practices to which they are exposed is deliberately hidden from them.

"This is the way things are" is the refrain. They are neither required nor encouraged to examine the situations in which they find themselves in a critical or evaluative manner. They are just supposed to learn about the "facts of life".

Uncritical and unquestioning practice is certainly not education. Yet, it is the fate of a large portion of our children in school.

### 4. THE NEED TO MAKE BIAS EXPLICIT

The kind of education we advocate has another requirement – the recognition that no education can be value-free or unbiased. The attempt to portray education as neutral or free of values is an attempt to mislead.

Every question asked implies others not asked. Every way of formulating a question leads more easily to some answers than others. Every "fact" is only one among many. Bias is inescapably a product of whatever a teacher does or does not do; whatever a textbook covers or does not cover; whatever a curriculum guideline recommends or fails to recommend.

Let's take an example. One can study racism as an academic exercise. One can also focus a lesson on the need to eliminate racism and explore ways to do so. Or, one can argue that the topic of racism has no room in the curriculum.

Each is a biased decision. Each is a political choice. Each has educational, philosophical and moral consequences.

No aspect of education avoids this issue. It is a thoroughly biased decision for an English teacher to discuss the minutiae of Shakespeare's plays but find no time to talk about the fundamental inequality in Shakespeare's England and its implications for contemporary Anglo-Canadian society.

Equally biased is a kindergarten or first grade program that finds no time to introduce children to the diversity of work and workers in their own community.

While the list could go on and on, the point is simple. Good education does not mean the rooting out of bias – an impossibility in any case – but rather making the teacher's and program's biases explicit so they can be the subject of critical examination and questioning and be an integral part of the learning process.

Learning how to think and learning how to learn for oneself requires the kind of critical reflection that is destroyed by the mystification of value-less learning.

What separates indoctrination from education is not the presence of bias in the teacher but the openness of the curriculum to critical thought and the attempt to pursue inquiry rigorously and fairly.

## 5. EQUALITY OF RESULTS

Education is a life-long process. It does not begin nor end in school. Yet, schooling is an indispensable phase of learning. Given the enormous resources that our province puts into the school system, we have every right to expect that system to play a significant role for everyone.

Children bring a diversity of backgrounds and experiences to kindergarten. When children leave school, we have every right to expect that they have gotten something tangible.

It is not acceptable to say we have provided all children with an equal opportunity to learn; for we have not. Those kids put in the lower streams in first grade are likely to stay there until they leave school. Despite everyone's best intentions, they had no equality of opportunity. Nor has there been equality of opportunity for girls and women in our educational system. They continue to be under-represented in a number of programs.

And it does not do to blame their failure on parents or on cultural backgrounds.

Of course, some kids come to school better prepared than others. But the whole point of a universal educational system that absorbs so much of the province's total budget is to equalize those differences.

The goal must be an equality of results, not of opportunity. Saying this does not mean a lockstep education through which everyone is forced. But it does mean recognition that there are skills and information that every person needs to function at home, in the community and at work.

It is our obligation to identify what these are and to pursue to the best of our ability the goal of making sure that everyone has these by the time they leave full-time schooling.

## 6. EDUCATION IS COLLECTIVE

Finally, we feel it is necessary to point out what follows from most of the preceding. Education is always a collective undertaking. We learn from each other, and no learning event occurs except as a result of a collective effort – of teacher and student, of writer and reader, of scholar and colleagues, etc.

Yet, we persist in structuring much of our schooling based on a notion of individualistic learning, often fostered through competition.

Were we to explicitly recognize the collective character of learning, we would find it much easier to plan teaching strategies that include everyone, that foster the notion that everyone has something to contribute to each task, and that create a climate of mutual support and help that would assist the fuller education of all learners.

## *CONCLUSION*

Our vision of the educational system is a challenging one. Not only do we feel it can be put into practice, we feel it must be.

We have avoided making programmatic suggestions in this presentation since that is reserved for later hearings. Suffice it to note that all the necessary elements to implement our approach to education are known and practised in one place or another.

The challenge that faces this committee, and all of us, is to have the courage to accept appropriate goals for our educational system. Once we have done this, we can turn to the equally challenging task of implementing those goals.

While this discussion may seem to many to be unnecessarily philosophical, it is wholly practical as well. The well-being of ourselves, our children and society depends on how we resolve these issues.

*Appendix II*

# "A SCHOOL AS A PLACE OF CELEBRATION IN WHICH CHILDREN ACQUIRE A PASSION FOR LEARNING AND CAN DEVELOP TO THEIR FULL POTENTIAL ... NEED NOT BE INCONSISTENT WITH HAVING A CORE CURRICULUM."

SUBMISSION TO
THE ONTARIO SELECT COMMITTEE ON EDUCATION
FROM THE ONTARIO FEDERATION OF LABOUR
OCTOBER 11, 1988

## INTRODUCTION

When we appeared before this committee in July, we identified a number of our major concerns with the education system in Ontario. We asked to have an opportunity to return to talk about what we see as solutions to those problems. We are pleased that you have provided us with that opportunity.

Our task is made easier because many of the essential changes that are necessary have already been identified in the report prepared for the Minister of Education by George Radwanski.

While there are a number of items in Radwanski's report with which we disagree, we feel that key items in that report provide the kind of blueprint which should guide this committee's recommendations.

There are six interrelated changes that we feel must be made in Ontario's educational system.

**1.** An end to streaming at both the elementary and secondary school levels.

**2.** A clear differentiation between "opportunity" and "outcome" in education and a commitment to the responsibility of the schools to bring all students to a high level of knowledge and skills regardless of background or initial interest.

**3.** A core curriculum – applicable to all children – that is designed to insure that all students have acquired the necessary skills and knowledge to function in our society by the time they have completed secondary school.

**4.** The development of new approaches to teaching and teacher training that will assist teachers in achieving the goals of the educational system.

**5.** The establishment of better methods to make the educational system accountable for meeting its objectives with regard to individual students as well as the society at large.

**6.** Integration of the community into the education system.

## *STREAMING*

The need to eliminate streaming from Ontario's elementary and secondary schools is a prerequisite to any kind of meaningful improvement in the educational system.

By "streaming", we are referring to the practice of dividing students into instructional groups on the criterion of assumed similarity in ability or attainment. This practice is sometimes referred to as "tracking", "ability grouping" and "homogeneous grouping."

Streaming starts in Ontario in elementary school and is formalized in Grade Nine. In our view the damage of streaming is done by the time children are formally streamed in secondary school.

The practice is so widespread that it is taken for granted as being an appropriate way to teach. Yet, the voluminous evidence on streaming does not support this conclusion.

Since this evidence has already been brought before you in the submissions of the Ontario English Catholic Teachers Federation and the Ontario Federation of Students, among others, we will not do so again.

We want simply to quote the summary of this evidence in the Radwanski Report: "The evidence now is overwhelming that streaming is a social injustice, a theoretical error and a practical failure." (p. 152)

Radwanski makes two recommendations regarding streaming. For elementary schools, he recommends:

> 19. That the practice of homogeneous ability grouping for instruction in any subject be discontinued by all schools in Ontario and, if necessary to achieve this result, that it be expressly prohibited by the Ministry of Education.(p. 134)

For secondary schools, he recommends:

> 27. That the current policy of streaming high school students into academic, general and basic courses of study be abolished, and

replaced by provision of a single and undifferentiated high-quality educational stream for all students. (p. 163)

Like us, Radwanski sees the elimination of streaming to be a prerequisite of any fundamental reform. He argues that

> doing away with streaming must lie at the heart of any strategy to address the fundamental need for improvements in our education system, to significantly reduce the dropout rate in the long run, and to provide meaningful educational outcomes for all our young people. **No recommendation in this report should be regarded as more important.** (p. 163, our emphasis)

Eliminating the practice of streaming will be difficult. A good deal of conventional pedagogical wisdom assumes the value of streaming. Most teachers in Ontario have been trained to teach using ability grouping. The entire secondary curriculum is premised on a streamed system.

Defenders of streaming use the rhetoric of "meeting each student's individual needs" to justify the practice.

In short, much of the educational bureaucracy in Ontario (like elsewhere) is so thoroughly wedded to streaming that its abolition seems unthinkable. The difficulty many had in responding to the Radwanski Report was due in part to their shock at his central attack on streaming.

But streaming must be eliminated from Ontario's schools. Whatever the laudable intentions of those who defend streaming, the reality is that streaming has been central to the perpetuation of a class-biased educational system that discriminates against working class and poor children.

The fact of class-bias – that working class and poor children do significantly worse than children of the well-to-do regardless of their abilities – is not a matter for debate. The empirical evidence is clear on this point.

It does not take a researcher to see the obvious. All you need do is visit any lower-stream secondary school. Every one is populated almost exclusively with working class and poor children.

Or, visit any so-called "special education" program other than those for the "gifted" or physically disabled, and you will find a similar pattern.

Although a moment ago we promised not to review the research once again, we must look at one study to illustrate our point. Careful research carried out by the Toronto Board of Education has shown that working class children were nine times more likely to be placed in non-physically disabled special education classes than middle class children. Further, middle class children who happened to be placed in these special education classes were 20 times more likely to get out of them than their working class counterparts.

If this committee does nothing else, it must demand the elimination of streaming from Ontario's schools. The sheer injustice of streaming should persuade you even if the educational failure of the practice does not.

The focus of the attack on streaming must begin in the elementary years. Unless streaming is eliminated there, it will not make any difference what is done at the high school level.

It is equally important to recognize that streaming which occurs within a classroom is every bit as pernicious as streaming which occurs by the division of children into different levels of schools.

Of course, the elimination of streaming will require many other changes. We will discuss these in subsequent sections.

## "OPPORTUNITY" AND "OUTCOME"

Our educators have long held "equality of opportunity" for all children as a goal for our educational system. However laudable that objective, it has been clear for many years that we are failing to achieve it. In practice, this language serves as a cover for class-biased streaming (including many forms of "special education"). It justifies this streaming through an ideology which says students with a wide range of abilities and backgrounds ought to have the opportunity of getting the best education of which they are capable.

The manifest failure of these class-biased "equal opportunity" arrangements are clear in the research literature and are clear to anyone who visits such programs.

The fact that socio-economic status may be the best predictor of one's placement in the streaming system and of one's ultimate educational attainment tells us that the school system is not providing equality of opportunity but rather reproducing the status positions from which the students come.

There are real costs as a result of this. Obviously, the student who ends up in a dead end program loses – as does his or her family. The wider society loses because talents and abilities of the dead-ended students are not developed. It also loses because a democracy suffers with an ill-informed and alienated citizenry.

Quite frankly, we are troubled by recent attempts to portray the problems of our educational system as essentially economic problems – linked primarily to the country's competitive position. We need better education for all, we are frequently told, so we can beat the Germans or the Americans or the Japanese in the world's marketplace. This position largely misses the point about what is happening to workers in our society. With new technology and work organization producing an increasingly pear-shaped distribution of jobs – the great majority requiring less and less skill and a much smaller minority requiring more skill – it is by no means clear we can justify better mass education on economic terms.

Here again, we would draw your attention to George Radwanski's views, in spite of his emphasis on making Canada's economy competitive. "It would ... be a grave mistake", he says, "to think that the importance of education in today's world is limited to matters of dollars and cents."

"The effective functioning of our democratic system of government, and hence the overall quality of life enjoyed by all our citizens, depends increasingly on having a knowledgeable and well-educated population. (p. 21)"

The justification for a good education for everyone ultimately rests on social, not economic, grounds.

We must talk about "outcome" and not "opportunity" if we are to change the class-based inequality of our present educational system.

The objective of schooling should be that, by the completion of high school, every student should have acquired the requisite knowledge and skills to function meaningfully in our society.

Like Radwanski, we find it unacceptable to justify Ontario's present practice of saying that what a child needs to know by the end of high school depends on whether he or she is going to university, to community college or directly into the work force.

If anything, students going into the work force need to have learned more, not less, in high school because that will likely be their last exposure to formal education.

To make a key point explicit, we reject the traditional view of the educational system as a funnel to higher education for some, with the rest left behind as "failures."

Our commitment to equality of outcome requires a belief that schools can overcome the differences with which children enter the system. Defenders of the status quo often deny this possibility – complaining that schools cannot be expected to make up for the inadequacies of the home and the parents. Given the enormous resources we put into our school system, this is an appalling apology for failure. It is also not true.

Schooling can bring all students to a level of adequate education for life in our society. A recent study by Paul Olson at the Ontario Institute for Studies in Education speaks clearly to this issue. In a careful ethnography of different classes in different schools, Olson concludes:

> It has been argued that schools cannot compensate for inequalities manifest in the larger society. Certainly such inequalities are powerful barriers to learning outcomes. But to assume that classrooms do not vary in their own success based on how creatively they use their own environments and abilities of teachers to teach is to miss important empirical differences in how classrooms can be places of learning regardless of exogenous factors.
>
> Spruce Grove [one site of Olson's research] is a transfusion of the educational soul precisely because it illustrates how much can be accomplished with skillful, caring teaching even with the most difficult of groups...
>
> MacDougall [a second site of Olson's research] is the practical consequence of a false sense of sophistication that knows what poor and working class kids can do and tries then to patronizingly 'compensate' for this. But this compensation is never heart felt. It is, instead, an exercise in determining what should be done for 'other peoples' children.
>
> ... by learning what works, by learning to share responsibilities and to integrate levels of curricular practice, a classroom comes together where discipline and failure are not the order of the day.

It is essential that this committee recommend commitment to a goal that all children, by the end of high school, have achieved the knowledge and skills necessary to function meaningfully in our society. It is also essential that you explicitly affirm the ability of schools to achieve this goal.

### *CORE CURRICULUM*

It follows necessarily from the foregoing that there must be a core curriculum for all students. A good common education for all children requires centralized curriculum development at the level of the province. We cannot achieve our preceding goal if we leave decision-making about the common core to the local school boards.

The importance of history or math or geography or languages is no different in Windsor or Kenora or Cornwall. And, with our mobile population, a student today in North Bay may be living tomorrow in Toronto or Kitchener or Thunder Bay.

As a province, we should identify what core curriculum we want all children to learn by the time they leave school. And we should develop the curricular materials, pedagogy, and teaching and learning conditions so that goal can be achieved.

The decision about the core curriculum will be a matter of some debate. We disagree, for example, with the elitist implications of some of Radwanski's suggested curriculum items. But we are in agreement that there must be a core and that the content of that should be determined after wide consultation.

We want to answer the criticism of some who oppose the notion of a core curriculum. Lloyd Dennis counterposes the notion of core curriculum with the view of a school as a place of celebration in which children acquire a passion for learning and can develop to their full potential.

Surely this view need not be inconsistent with having a core curriculum. A passion for learning comes from having committed and caring teachers whose own love for learning is transmitted to the students. It also comes from challenging and interesting tasks that are seen as relevant to the children's lives.

Neither of these requisites has any necessary relationship to particular courses. The teaching of Shakespeare can be an ordeal of boring irrelevance, or it can be an occasion of excitement and discovery. So can the teaching of auto mechanics or physics or art.

But without a core curriculum, a significant number of children will leave the educational system without the knowledge they will need to participate actively and fully in society.

Likewise, we would like to dispel the concern that a provincially-set curriculum means there is no role for local input.

Specific reading material should be relevant to the lives of the learners – a point made well in the brief submitted to you by the Ontario Federation of Students. Equally, teachers' explanations of why various subjects are important should reflect the real world out of which their students come.

It is not conducive to learning to use materials or approaches that have no resonance with the students' lives. And lives, we want to stress, can be different in Dryden than in London; and different again in Toronto's Regent Park than in Rosedale a few blocks away.

Our point is that while the subjects and the level of attainment should be set provincially, the materials and approaches to achieve those goals should have significant local input.

In addition, local input regarding pedagogical techniques is a necessary supplement to general pedagogical training that would be common province-wide.

Finally, there would have to be significant local determination of the kinds and extent of tutoring programs necessary to help students reach the designated level of attainment.

We feel strongly that the current credit system should be eliminated as part of the move to a common curriculum. Radwanski provides a catalogue of the problems with the credit system in Ontario [see pp. 169 - 171].

However progressive a credit system may seem, we feel it has reactionary consequences. It provides advantages to those students whose parents are more familiar with the educational system and can advise their children which courses to take. It pits teachers against each other in attracting "good" students to optional courses. It works against the provision of breadth and local relevance as a necessary feature of all courses.

It is our conviction that any formal elimination of streaming would be entirely undone by maintenance of the credit system.

The objectives of variety, relevance and inherent interest to each student can be achieved through the teaching approaches by which a common curriculum is delivered and in the selection of materials to be used. While some optional courses should be available in grades 11 and 12, they should be subordinate to achieving success in the core curriculum.

A core curriculum in which the same students would be together for most subjects provides a partial antidote to the alienation and impersonality that marks high school education under the credit system. It would also increase the likelihood that teachers would get to know their students better and be better able to use the dynamics of the group as part of their teaching approach.

## *PEDAGOGY AND TEACHER TRAINING*

The changes we are proposing have profound pedagogical implications. Since we understand that the Committee may have further hearings to deal with issues of pedagogy, we will reserve most of our remarks for that time.

Now, we want simply to point to some key suggestions. On the one hand, our view of good pedagogy is that which creates a supportive task-oriented environment that is authentically interactive and challenging to children.

How to achieve this is a matter of considerable complexity. Certain requisites are clear. There will have to be a significant increase in resources for teachers. The approach to education we are proposing requires a substantial amount of time, good teaching conditions, creative teacher training, and interesting and relevant learning materials.

One obvious necessity is a significant reduction in class sizes. This has implications for the number of teachers to be trained, the availability of classrooms, etc. To some extent, this reduction can be made easier by the redeployment of many non-classroom teachers to the classroom.

A second necessity will be the provision of more preparation time for teachers. University teachers are only required to be in the classroom six to nine hours a week because of the recognition of the time it takes to prepare for a class. If anything, we feel the demands on an elementary or secondary teacher – attempting to meet the individual needs of 20-30 diverse students – is as difficult a task as giving a university lecture. More time must be allotted our teachers to meet the demands we are placing on them.

A third requirement is revised teacher training that equips teachers with the ability to teach effectively without "ability grouping." Such techniques are known and used in a variety of schools. These must become a central part of "pre-service" training and ongoing "in-service" training.

One particular approach which we feel merits wider use is "cooperative learning" groups. This approach to teaching breaks up a heterogeneous class of students into interdependent (and still heterogeneous) groups where learning goals link group members. In addition to cooperative task structures, there are cooperative reward structures which encourage students to help each other learn.

There is a wealth of good research material which shows that this approach to learning results in significant gains for all students when compared with traditional individualized, competitive teaching strategies. The gains are not only in the amount students learn, in their motivation to learn more and in the confidence they acquire, but also in gains in increased empathy for others, in reduced intergroup tension and aggression and in more tolerance of ethnic and racial diversity.

A fourth requirement is increased emphasis on teachers teaching what they know and like. Assigning a physical education teacher to teach math or an English teacher to teach social studies goes against what we know about learning. Teachers are best able to motivate students to learn when their own enthusiasm for the subject comes through to the student.

One implication of this requirement is that there should be greater emphasis on training teachers in their own subject, thus shifting the current one-sided focus on methodology. Teachers should also have the opportunity for regular sabbaticals in order to pursue further study in their own subject fields.

While these recommendations have major financial implications, there are even more significant costs to our society associated with the present school system. Ultimately, we are going to have to decide whether we want to put more of our money up front to help create meaningful lives for our students or whether we want to continue to bear the long-term social and personal costs engendered by the current system.

## ACCOUNTABILITY

A major concern of many with our educational system is its lack of accountability. "How", it is often asked, "can a child complete Grade 12 without knowing how to read and write?"; "How are we to know if we are getting value for our educational dollar?"

A quick and superficial answer is the reintroduction of standardized, province-wide testing. Radwanski, along with many others, adopts this approach.

We think this is a bad idea which would do more harm than good. The issue of accountability is central to us, but standardized provincial testing will not achieve anything useful for students or teachers or parents. One need only look at the United States to see an educational system in which such testing is widely practised and where the problems make ours pale by comparison.

As we surely should have learned from Ontario's historical experience with standardized provincial testing, educational programs are inevitably skewed to doing well on the tests. In its worst form, the entire curriculum is twisted to anticipating what the testers will be asking the students and nothing else.

While many students may demonstrate "knowledge" because their teachers are good at guessing what will be on the tests, there is no necessary relationship between the test score and any meaningful learning.

Further, we know that a variety of people do poorly on tests even when they know the subject. Cultural biases in tests, psychological variations in testing situations, and a host of exogenous factors can significantly affect test results in a manner that has no relationship to knowledge of the subject being tested.

While there are no easy answers to the issue of accountability, there are answers. At the level of the individual student, more effort must be put into equipping teachers with the ability and the commitment to communicating a student's progress fully and accurately to parents. This often requires overcoming parents' intimidation by educational authorities, cultural differences in modes of expression between parents and teachers, and parents' unfamiliarity with educational jargon.

A good teacher has a solid understanding of how each student is doing. We must find ways for that information to be communicated more clearly to those who share responsibility for the student's life. A review of these techniques might be a valuable appendix to this committee's final report. We in the labour movement would be most interested in participating in the creation of such a document.

At the level of the Board and the Province, there are a host of ways of evaluating how the curriculum is being implemented and whether the objectives of the curriculum are being met.

At a broader level, the education system must be accountable for its goal of adequately educating everyone. We do not need standardized testing of students to realize the failure of the system in this regard. The statistics cited in the debate on streaming make it apparent that the school system is not succeeding in providing a good education for all students regardless of ethnic, class or racial background.

This level of accountability is relatively easy to measure. The Ministry of Education should draft specific equity goal statements and establish a social audit mechanism to determine on a regular basis whether these equity goals are being met.

## *COMMUNITY INVOLVEMENT*

While much of the thrust of our recommendations is to strengthen centralized responsibility for education, there is a more active role for the community.

As we recognize the demands our recommendations will be placing on our teachers, we should move to lighten their load by involving the community more actively in fulfilling non-teaching responsibilities currently done by teachers or not done at all.

The resources of each school's community must be drawn upon to enrich the extra-curricular opportunities available to students. Programs must be encouraged to involve local artists or craftspeople or tradespeople or athletes or writers.

The resources of the community should be assessed by each school's administration, and teachers should be made aware of these and encouraged to take advantage of the resources in planning their lessons.

This is a very different approach to that found within many of our boards which attempt to substitute volunteers for union labour in essential service activities.

Closer community links also must be promoted by encouragement of more active parent involvement in the school system. Parental involvement must be more than requesting information about one's own child or helping raise money through the school's fundraising drive.

Real parent involvement will require leadership from the Ministry in the form of support for school-community relations departments in each board. These departments should be charged with getting parents more actively involved. In essence they would work for the parents. The model should be that of the Toronto Board's SCR Department before it was dismantled by a hostile Board threatened by the real parental involvement the Department had helped achieve.

While boards and administrators may want parents to leave the school system to the "professionals", the Province must make clear that real parental involvement can only strengthen the educational system.

Finally, the link between the community and school must be strengthened by a provincial directive which requires boards to make school facilities available to non-profit community groups at no cost. The entire community underwrites the cost of the school and the entire community should have access to school facilities as long as that access does not interfere with regular school functions.

## *CONCLUSION*

Debates about our educational system generate a good deal of interest because of the importance that system has to our society.

We expect it to be the place where children learn to think critically and creatively, learn how to learn and learn to want to learn. On the other hand, we also feel it is the place where children must learn the requisite skills and knowledge to participate fully in our society – at home, at work and in the community.

These two sets of objectives are sometimes seen as antithetical. They are not.

Our educational system has not done terribly well in meeting either of them. While the failure hurts the society generally, the brunt of the burden is borne by working class and poor children who comprise the majority of the "castoffs" of the educational system.

By re-examining our purposes and resolving to change practices that have produced our present failings, we can move our system forward. The recommendations of this committee will have a significant impact upon the future.

A reaffirmation of the need to educate everyone well is the starting point for change. Abolition of streaming, introduction of a core curriculum, new approaches to pedagogy and teacher training, better teaching conditions and materials, greater concern for real accountability and an increased role for the community are the prescription for significant improvement.

*Appendix III*

## "A STRONG PUBLIC EDUCATIONAL SYSTEM IS ESSENTIAL TO THE KIND OF SOCIETY WE IN THE LABOUR MOVEMENT WANT TO BUILD. IT WILL COST A GOOD DEAL OF MONEY."

SUBMISSION TO
THE ONTARIO SELECT COMMITTEE ON EDUCATION
FROM THE ONTARIO FEDERATION OF LABOUR,
SEPTEMBER 26, 1989

### INTRODUCTION

In our previous presentations to this committee, we have been very critical of the education system in Ontario. While we applauded its goals, we indicated a grave concern about its failure to provide good education to many Ontarians.

We recommended an end to streaming at both the elementary and secondary school level, a commitment to equality of outcome, a core curriculum, development and adoption of new approaches to teaching and teacher training, better measures for assuring the accountability of the educational system and more integration of the community into the educational system.

We are not alone in criticizing Ontario's schools. It has become a popular sport to bash the public educational system. Hardly a day goes by when there is not a statement by a business leader or an editorial in a major newspaper or a story by a concerned parent or advice from an educational expert about the inadequacies of the schools.

Many educators throw up their hands in despair – retreating into cynicism, animosity, or apathy.

But, it is important to distinguish among the critics, among the types of criticisms being voiced and among the solutions being offered.

Many, including much of the business community, want to return to an imaginary golden age when students learned the "basics" and were not inundated with "frills", when there were standardized tests to really measure what had been learned, when discipline and respect for authority were the hallmark of education, and when students emerged from school ready for work.

That "golden age" never existed. Education in the past was a poor cousin to the present. The past is a desirable model only to those with foggy memories or who are ignorant of history.

Reference to this fictional past serves a purpose. It provides a basis for advocacy of change that would perpetuate the inequalities of the present. It gives credence to solutions that would further entrench a system already too elitist, too discriminatory to the working class, too focused on meeting employers needs, too unconcerned with meeting the requirement of producing an informed and critical citizenry – essential to our survival as a democracy and as a world.

This fictional past is used to rationalize an attack on public education – an attack that finds solutions in some form of increased private sector involvement in education.

## A COMMITMENT TO PUBLIC EDUCATION
## DEEPENED BY CRITICISM

The labour movement's criticism of the educational system has often been lumped in with these other critics. We want to dissociate ourselves from them – again.

Unlike them, our commitment to the public educational system is deepened by our criticism. We feel that more resources must be put into that system to allow it to grow stronger and more responsive to the needs of everyone in our society.

We do not see teachers as laggards who need a good dose of exposure to the so-called "real" world – as if having to teach 35 boisterous eight-year-olds is less the "real" world than slinging hamburgers at McDonalds or being an accountant at First Canadian Place or selling stocks on Bay Street or managing a bakery in Timmins.

We see teachers as hard-working, dedicated people who have the real interests of their students at heart, but who often are not given good enough training and who increasingly have to perform under impossible working conditions with inadequate materials.

We feel that the integrity of the public educational system (in Ontario in 1989 that means both the public and Roman Catholic elementary and secondary schools, community colleges and universities) must be protected from those who want to preserve their private privilege through gaining public money for private schools – whether through direct funding, through providing "vouchers" or by any other means that compromises the public commitment to an exclusively public system.

We also feel that the integrity of the public system also must be protected from private interests who want to use the public schools for their private advantage. The goal of elementary and secondary education is not to serve employers. It is not to assure that exiting students are job-ready. It is not to sort people so universities know whom to admit. It is not to stratify the population so the current social hierarchy is preserved.

The integrity of the public educational system is compromised by efforts to give private interests privileged access to schools whether this be through business-industry-education councils, "adopt-a-school" programs [the notion that public schools are available for private "adoption" is repugnant] or other programs that have a similar effect. We must find ways to involve the community more fully in the educational system – but the whole community, not privileged segments of it.

The purpose of our school system must be to educate everybody so that they are better able to participate fully and influentially in all aspects of their lives – at home, at work and in the community. It is to equip everybody with the ability to learn how to learn, to think critically and to be able to act on their views.

## *SUPPORTING EDUCATION WITH A VISION OF SOCIAL RESPONSIBILITY*

Getting increased public support for public education with these goals will be difficult in the current political climate dominated by the business agenda that stresses international competition, less public initiative, smaller government, and private privilege.

The real commitment to genuine public education grows out of a vision of collective social responsibility, of collective good, of collective survival or collective destruction. We criticize the public educational system because we realize that a strong public educational system is essential to the kind of society we in the labour movement want to build. It will cost a good deal of money to implement the changes we have advocated in previous briefs.

We strongly support the expenditure of that money.

Other critics have a different view. Prime Minister Mulroney claims the educational system is central to his vision of Canada while at the same time arguing that "urgent need for improvements...would not be solved with money from the Federal Government, urging instead that more study and more private sector effort be put into the problems." We assume he is referring to the private sector in which only one out of four employers provides any training for its workers, and most of that training ignores much of what is known about good educational practice.

The Premier's Council in Ontario, dominated by corporate voices, complains that "the education system in Ontario is not delivering value for the money it receives." We feel just the opposite: Ontario does not provide enough money for the kind of educational system we value.

The statistics are clear. In 1975, the provincial share of total education costs in Ontario was 61 percent. By 1988, this had dropped to 48 percent. Ninety percent of the school boards in Ontario are forced to exceed the provincial grant ceilings in order to offer the education they presently provide. The stories of the effects of underfunding the educational system are many: thirty-five children in elementary school classes, decaying buildings, school yards filled with portables, ridiculously small library budgets, children having to sell candy to raise money for necessary school equipment, students having to share textbooks because there are not enough to go around. Any teacher or school board administrator appearing before you can add many other examples.

With the growing demands being placed on the educational system, with the rapid social and economic changes engulfing Canada, with the cultural and social diversity of our population, we cannot have the kind of educational system everyone claims to want without much more substantial funding. The Prime Minister and his business colleagues are wrong if they think the problem can be solved by a hard-nosed private-sector approach to cost cutting. Most school boards with which we are familiar could give the business community a few lessons on how to stretch a dollar.

Unlike private sector businesses, school boards, fortunately, cannot decide to make their budgets go further by moving operations to South Carolina or Mexico or Taiwan. Equally fortunately, they are prevented from saving money, like private schools, by refusing to admit those who are more difficult or require more of the teacher's time. Financial pressure and private sector ideology are prompting some boards to adopt short-sighted private sector business practices like contracting out necessary services, moving to school-based budgeting and shifting non-teaching staff work to part-time and temporary employees.

## *SUFFICIENT AND EQUITABLE FUNDING*

While there are undoubtedly ways in which some money can be better spent by school boards, the fact is that they do not have enough funding to meet the tasks which they should properly be undertaking. Funding for education must be increased. There is no acceptable alternative.

This raises a second matter. Not only must education funding be increased, it must also be raised in a more equitable way. As the provincial share of funding falls, school boards are forced to turn to property taxpayers to make up the difference. The extreme case is Metropolitan Toronto where the Provincial Government contributes nothing to the cost of education. The entire $1,678,000,000 is paid by taxpayers through the regressive property tax. On average, 52% of the cost of education in Ontario is paid by local taxes on property.

We recommend that education be funded entirely by the province and that this money be raised by more progressive corporate and personal income taxes. Taxes for education should be related to one's ability to pay.

## *CONCLUSION*

We want a real end to the class-biased practice of homogeneous "ability" grouping in elementary years and formal streaming in secondary schools [not the cosmetic change this committee recommended in its earlier report]. We want better training for teachers, and we want them to have the materials, preparation time and working conditions that allow them to help our children learn more effectively.

We strongly support smaller classes, universal junior kindergarten programs, full day senior kindergartens, child care centres in all schools.

We want innovative ways to involve parents and the community in all aspects of education.

We support special funding for francophone programs, for heritage languages, for programs to integrate disabled children into regular classes, for necessary capital needs.

This all will require a more significant commitment to education and a more significant commitment to increased funding. Right now our educational system discriminates against working class students by disproportionately bottom-streaming them – dumping them out of school without the skills and abilities they need.

It discriminates against working class parents by forcing them to pay a disproportionate share of educational costs as a result of increasingly funding education out of regressive property taxes.

We want this committee to make the hard recommendations necessary to change these two realities. We hope you have the courage to do so.

# JOIN THE DEBATE ON WHAT SHOULD HAPPEN IN CANADA'S SCHOOLS

The issues raised in books like this one will be carried on the pages of

## Our Schools/Our Selves
## A Magazine For Canadian Education Activists

The best way to keep in touch is to fill out of the subscription forms at the back and mail it in.

But we hope you'll do more than read us. We hope you'll get involved in these issues, if you aren't already.
And that you'll let us know what you think of our articles and books.

### FOR A YEAR'S SUBSCRIPTION YOU'LL GET 4 MAGAZINES AND 4 BOOKS.

The next issue of the magazine (December 1989) will include articles on:

Private School Funding – Racism in Nova Scotia Schools – Literacy in Mozambique – Privatizing our College System – Children of the State, Part II – School Consolidation in P.E.I. – Workers and the Rise of Mass Schooling – The Manitoba High School Review – Trading-in Saskatchewan's Trade Schools – High Schools and Teen Age Sex – CUPE's Educational Agenda

## In the first three years of Our Schools/Our Selves you will have received the following books:

- Ken Osborne, **Educating Citizens: A Democratic Socialist Agenda for Canadian Education**
- La Maîtresse d'école, **Building a People's Curriculum: The Experience of a Quebec Teachers' Collective**
- Jane Gaskell, Arlene McLaren, Myra Novogrodsky, **Claiming an Education: Feminism and Canadian Schools**
- Jim Turk, ed., **Labour, Education, and Skill Training**
- Jim Cummins, Marcel Danesi, **The Development and Denial of Canada's Linguistic Resources**
- Loren Lind, **Their Rightful Place: The Childcare Issue in Canada**
- Célestin Freinet, **Techniques of Cooperative Learning**
- Ken Osborne, **The Politics of Teaching: A Democratic Socialist Approach to Pedagogy in Canadian Schools**
- Bruce Kidd, **Kids, Sports, and the Body: A Feminist Socialist Approach to Physical Education**
- William Bruneau, David Clandfield, **Where Does The NDP Stand in Education?**
- Doug Noble, **The Military/Corporate Agenda in North American Education**
- Celia Haig-Brown, Robert Regnier, ed., **A Strategy for Native Education in Canada**

*The subscription price for each of these books will be as much as 50% off the bookstore price.*

## Subscribe Today And Give A Subscription Form To A Friend